# INVESTMENT
# CLUBS

*A* Team Approach

to the

Stock Market

## Kathryn Shaw

Dearborn
Financial Publishing, Inc.

While a great deal of care has been taken to provide accurate and current information, the ideas, suggestions, general principles and conclusions presented in this text are subject to local, state and federal laws and regulations, court cases and any revisions of same. The reader is thus urged to consult legal counsel regarding any points of law—this publication should not be used as a substitute for competent legal advice.

Senior Associate Editor: Karen A. Christensen
Managing Editor: Jack Kiburz
Associate Project Editor: Stephanie C. Schmidt
Cover Design: Design Alliance, Inc.
Interior Design: Lucy Jenkins

Published by Dearborn Financial Publishing, Inc.

Printed in the United States of America

95 96 97 10 9 8 7 6 5 4 3 2


**Library of Congress Cataloging-in-Publication Data**

Shaw, Kathryn, 1937–
    Investment clubs : a team approach to the stock market / Kathryn Shaw.
        p.   cm.
    Includes index.
    ISBN 0-7931-1345-8 (pbk.)
    1. Investment clubs—United States—Management. 2. Stocks—United States. 3. Speculation—United States.   I. Title.
HG4930.S463   1995
332.63′22—dc20                                                            95-2893
                                                                                    CIP

# CONTENTS

# PREFACE

$\mathcal{E}$ight years ago, a friend and I heard that investment clubs are a smart way for someone with limited financial resources to become involved in the stock market, so we decided to start a club. After some false starts, we began the Women's Investment Club with seven members and $700. Today, our membership has increased to 20 and our initial $700 has grown to approximately $40,000.

The first modern-day investment club began in Detroit in the 1940s. Each founding member of that club, having invested $20 to $25 every month, had by the early 1980s accumulated over $200,000! Whenever I hear this story, I wish I had joined an investment club sooner.

Some of you may be hesitant to get involved in a club because you know nothing about investing in the stock market. But that, too, is why you should join or start an investment club. Most of us don't have the self-discipline to learn on our own. Besides, it's much easier and more fun to learn together and share investment knowledge.

I've spent the past few years talking to people about their personal finances, and I've discovered that most of you are seeking additional ways to make money. Investment clubs provide that opportunity. *Investment Clubs: A Team Approach to the Stock Market* shows you how easy it is to start your own club. It explains all the details you must address so that your club can operate successfully, including how to set up your club's business structure and what legal requirements you must satisfy before your club can begin investing. Using this book can help your investment club avoid the painful trial-and-error period my club experienced.

I'm constantly asked how to join an existing club or how to find people interested in forming one. To help existing clubs find new members and those people find others interested in starting their own, I've included a sheet for you to copy at the back of this book. If you are already a member of an investment club and your club would like to expand its membership, please complete the sheet and send it to me. If you are one of the many who are seeking ways to make money and want to start an investment club, you too should complete this sheet. I will keep your names on file for two years, and with your responses I will create a database of would-be members so that I can notify those of you living in the same geographic area of one another.

Stocks are the only investment vehicle I discuss for investment clubs. Certainly, some clubs invest in real estate and bonds, but it has been well documented that clubs with the best long-term record are those that invest in the stock market. You'll find no advice on how to select stocks or stock mutual funds, however; dozens of useful books are already available on the subject. This book's strength is its step-by-step approach to setting up an investment club.

Like the other members in the Women's Investment Club, I believe that *everyone* should become knowledgeable in matters of investing, so this book is written for *every* potential investor. Many happy investment returns!

# ACKNOWLEDGMENTS

$\mathcal{A}$ number of people and organizations have contributed to this undertaking. First and foremost, I thank the Women's Investment Club for providing the experiences necessary to write this book. Our club's broker, Barbara Bensley of the A. G. Edwards & Sons, Inc., brokerage firm, deserves credit for suggesting this project. I am deeply indebted to Barb for her help and for enthusiastically sharing her investment knowledge with us. I thank our club's first treasurer, Carolyn Noland, for patiently teaching us an accounting system that has been developed for investment clubs. Our club's present co-treasurer, Sharon Glenn, has reviewed my illustrations and opened my eyes to all the details involved in her job. I am especially grateful to my friend and fellow club member, Trish Fiebing, who spent two years gently prodding and encouraging me while offering valuable criticism and worthwhile suggestions. I thank Louise Hagerty who has, unknowingly, taught me perseverance. Susan Bondy, too, deserves credit for reviewing my manuscript and offering useful advice. I also appreciate Nathaniel Stroup's interest and assistance. Two important organizations must be mentioned: The National Association of Investors Corporation, more commonly known as the NAIC, and the American Association of Individual Investors (AAII). Both organizations are wonderful resources for the beginning investor. The NAIC, in particular, is a valuable resource for investment clubs, and I have referred to this organization throughout the book. The AAII, too, offers the novice investor a wealth of information and benefits.

I thank Karen Christensen who has put her heart and soul into this book, making it easier to read. Of course, I must acknowledge my family's support and encouragement. My son, Colin Hall, spent precious free time sharing his writing and marketing skills with me, and my son-in-law, Mark Smith, has been particularly supportive. Last, but by no means least, I thank my mother, Jean; my husband, Bob; and my daughter, Sarah, for their confidence in me.

# Part One

# FORMING A DYNAMIC CLUB

Two stonecutters were asked what they
were doing. The first said,
"I'm cutting this stone into blocks."
The second replied,
"I'm on a team that's building
a cathedral."

*Anonymous*

CHAPTER 1

# GETTING STARTED!

$\mathcal{H}$ave you won the lottery? Are you a *Reader's Digest* sweepstakes winner? Or are you, like most of us, just trying to put aside a few dollars every month and wanting to watch your savings grow? It's a well-known fact that the stock market has, over time, outperformed all other types of investments. Yet, how many of us know anything about investing in the market? It would be great if stockbrokers spoke English instead of Greek. And how reassuring it would be if we could hold a broker's hand as we venture into the market without having to pay an arm and a leg. But you can learn how to invest in a way that's fun and rewarding and won't cost you a fortune—by starting your own investment club.

An investment club is a group of people, usually between 10 and 20, who meet at least once a month to increase their investment knowledge. They contribute a predetermined amount of money, which they then pool to invest, typically in the stock market. Generally, monthly contributions are modest, ranging between $20 and $50, with $25 to $30 being the average. Because these contributions are small, the investment club approach is a low-cost, affordable way to learn how to purchase stocks. And once you've gained some investment knowledge and confidence through a club experience, you can use the lessons you've learned to manage stocks in a portfolio of your own.

This book assumes you're a beginning investor with little or no stock market experience, and it outlines the mechanics of starting an investment club in four easy steps. By following these steps, you'll be able to quickly dispense with the often confusing and sometimes overwhelming organizational details of starting a club. Obviously, the sooner you complete these details, the sooner you can start the business of making money.

The book is divided into three parts: Forming a Dynamic Club, Operating for Success and Beginning To Invest Wisely. Part I describes the four steps necessary to organize your club. There's no particular period within which to complete these steps, but they will be easier to accomplish if you use the checklist found at the end of each step as an outline for items you must address at your meetings.

Part II discusses your club's operations and an accounting system that has been developed specifically for investment clubs. Further, you'll learn the information to include in your monthly financial reports, methods for expanding your membership and other topics vital to your club's success.

Part III explains how and where to begin your search for stocks to analyze. This section also gives you some trading techniques that are appropriate for investment clubs.

The appendixes include sample articles of association and a partnership agreement for you to adopt to meet the legal requirements of starting an investment club. You can adapt them to meet your club's specific needs. When you have decided which business structure to use, I recommend that you have an attorney review the proper document to ensure that it meets your state's regulations.

For all you would-be investors who want to own a share of the Dow, let's get started!

# Tips for Success

Share Your Enthusiasm

Be Persistent

Seek Members Who Have Something in Common

Start Small

# CHAPTER 2

# STEP ONE:
## Finding the Right Members

According to the National Association of Investors Corporation (NAIC), each of the approximately 50,000 investment clubs currently operating in the United States invests an average of $250 a month or $3,000 a year in the stock market. Imagine! If you had started your club ten years ago and had invested $3,000 in high-quality growth stocks your first year, today your $3,000 could be worth more than $9,000. The New York Stock Exchange estimates that one in five residents of the United States—a total of 51 million people—owns stocks or invests in stock mutual funds—and 51 million people can't be wrong! You don't have to be wealthy to start an investment club. So join a friend and begin your walk down Wall Street!

You'll soon discover that starting a club is a real challenge, a challenge that becomes easier once you find two or three kindred spirits who are as eager as you to form a club.

Membership is crucial to your club's success. You must re-
cruit individuals who feel a sense of responsibility for
making your club succeed. Talk to people who you think
may share your enthusiasm and desire to learn about investing in the stock market—people in your office, fellow
health club members or members of organizations to which
you belong. When you've recruited two or three prospective members, surely they'll be able to recommend
others who also share your enthusiasm and would like to
join your club. If you already have a stockbroker or know
one personally, he or she, too, may be able to recommend
some clients as candidates for membership. The types of
members who most likely can contribute to your club's
success are discussed in more detail in Chapter 3.

Figure 2.1 is a list on which to keep the names of current
members. It's important that all founding members have
this list so all can easily get in touch with one another. As
your club begins to grow, you also should keep a prospective member list (see Figure 2.2). You'll find that, while
many individuals may mention their desire to join your club
when there are no vacancies, you may have forgotten their
names and phone numbers when vacancies arise. By
keeping a list of your most current membership plus a list of
prospective members, you will be able to contact prospective members quickly to determine whether they still
wish to become involved. Regularly update these lists.

Another way to help you find prospective members is to
fill out the tear-out sheet at the back of this book. If you are
attempting to start a club or if your club is seeking additional members, complete this form and send it to the address indicated. We will add your name or your club's name
to a database of investment club enthusiasts, and we will
inform you of others in your geographical area who share
your interest. We will keep your name in this database for
two years after receiving notice of your investment club interest.

**FIGURE 2.1**    Member List

<table>
<tr><td colspan="3" align="center">**Members**</td></tr>
<tr><td>Date:</td><td></td><td></td></tr>
<tr><td>**Name**</td><td>**Address**</td><td>**Phone #**</td></tr>
<tr><td>_____</td><td>_____</td><td>h: _____</td></tr>
<tr><td></td><td>_____</td><td>w: _____</td></tr>
<tr><td></td><td>_____</td><td>f: _____</td></tr>
<tr><td>_____</td><td>_____</td><td>h: _____</td></tr>
<tr><td></td><td>_____</td><td>w: _____</td></tr>
<tr><td></td><td>_____</td><td>f: _____</td></tr>
<tr><td>_____</td><td>_____</td><td>h: _____</td></tr>
<tr><td></td><td>_____</td><td>w: _____</td></tr>
<tr><td></td><td>_____</td><td>f: _____</td></tr>
<tr><td>_____</td><td>_____</td><td>h: _____</td></tr>
<tr><td></td><td>_____</td><td>w: _____</td></tr>
<tr><td></td><td>_____</td><td>f: _____</td></tr>
<tr><td>_____</td><td>_____</td><td>h: _____</td></tr>
<tr><td></td><td>_____</td><td>w: _____</td></tr>
<tr><td></td><td>_____</td><td>f: _____</td></tr>
<tr><td>_____</td><td>_____</td><td>h: _____</td></tr>
<tr><td></td><td>_____</td><td>w: _____</td></tr>
<tr><td></td><td>_____</td><td>f: _____</td></tr>
<tr><td>_____</td><td>_____</td><td>h: _____</td></tr>
<tr><td></td><td>_____</td><td>w: _____</td></tr>
<tr><td></td><td>_____</td><td>f: _____</td></tr>
<tr><td>_____</td><td>_____</td><td>h: _____</td></tr>
<tr><td></td><td>_____</td><td>w: _____</td></tr>
<tr><td></td><td>_____</td><td>f: _____</td></tr>
</table>

Investment clubs come in all shapes, sizes and have different goals. No rules dictate how you should develop a cohesive membership or how many members your club should have. Clubs have a better success rate, however, if their members share a common thread. For example, I recently read of a club whose seven members are all part of one family. After starting with seven members, my club's membership is comprised of 20 women. Our club has held joint meetings with another club in our town whose eight members are teachers at the local high school. Ideally, the ultimate size of your club should range between 15 and 18 members, with 20 being the maximum. I recommend starting with seven or eight, however, because in the initial stages of organization, it is often difficult to make decisions with input from 15 to 20 members.

Starting your club with seven or eight friends or co-workers is more manageable and will give you time to build confidence in your ability to manage the club. Later, as you add new members, consider recruiting individuals who will bring complementary talents to your club. A prospective member who has managerial skills could make a good future president, while an individual who enjoys working with numbers could easily handle your club's financial responsibilities.

But for now, when you have a list of seven or eight people who are eager to join you in learning about the stock market, take the bull by the horns—start your own investment club!

**FIGURE 2.2**    Prospective Member List

**Prospective Members**

Date:

| Name | Address | Phone # |
|------|---------|---------|
| _____ | _____ | h: _____ |
| | _____ | w: _____ |
| | _____ | f: _____ |
| _____ | _____ | h: _____ |
| | _____ | w: _____ |
| | _____ | f: _____ |
| _____ | _____ | h: _____ |
| | _____ | w: _____ |
| | _____ | f: _____ |
| _____ | _____ | h: _____ |
| | _____ | w: _____ |
| | _____ | f: _____ |
| _____ | _____ | h: _____ |
| | _____ | w: _____ |
| | _____ | f: _____ |
| _____ | _____ | h: _____ |
| | _____ | w: _____ |
| | _____ | f: _____ |
| _____ | _____ | h: _____ |
| | _____ | w: _____ |
| | _____ | f: _____ |
| _____ | _____ | h: _____ |
| | _____ | w: _____ |
| | _____ | f: _____ |

# Tips for Success

Be Sure Members Are Committed

Invest Regularly

Don't Expect To Get Rich Quickly

Think Long Term

CHAPTER 3

# STEP TWO:
## Uncovering the
## Ingredients of Success

$\mathcal{N}$ow that you have found seven or eight people interested in forming your investment club, your next step is to call a meeting to discuss the following ingredients, which have proven essential to an investment club's success. At this meeting, you and your founding members should make sure that you share the same goals before your club opens for business.

## Discuss Your Members' Level of Commitment

Commitment is the most vital ingredient of your club's success. You and your founding members must recognize your responsibility to contribute not only money but, more importantly, time. Club meetings take approximately an hour and one-half to two hours each month, and members should plan to spend an additional two to three hours monthly reading and researching investment materials. How much time you spend in the learning process is up to you, but the more you read, the more you'll learn. At the very least, make a daily habit of reading the business section of your local newspaper and ease into *The Wall Street Journal*. The Journal publishes a special "Educational Edition" that teaches you how to read and use the newspaper. To order this special edition, call 800-568-7625. The Money section of *USA Today* also is educational and easy to understand.

Once you begin reading investment materials, you'll be amazed at how much you're learning, thereby becoming a valued member of your club.

## Form Your Club's Investment Philosophy

Investment philosophy is another important factor contributing to your club's success. Following are the three key elements of a successful investment philosophy: The types of stocks in which you invest, how often you invest and what you do with the earnings from your investments. As a group, discuss how these three keys form your club's investment philosophy.

### 1. Risk Levels

What types of stocks should you buy? The types of stocks you purchase will be directly related to members' *risk tolerance levels*—the amount of risk you're comfortable taking. Investing in stock involves risk, but there are degrees, or levels, of risk. Certainly, bungee jumping involves more risk than walking across the street, unless you live in New York City. The same analogy also applies to the stock market. Penny stocks, new issues or stocks emerging from a special situation such as Chapter 11 reorganization hold greater risk than do high-quality growth stocks. Individuals who want to invest only in penny stocks, at, say, $2 per share and who dream of selling these shares for $4 three months later should be discouraged from joining your club. One of the primary reasons investment clubs fail is that members lose interest when it becomes apparent that the club isn't going to make a fast fortune in the stock market.

One of the first stocks my club bought was a high-tech "flyer" recommended by a friend's broker. We bought the stock without doing a thorough analysis of the company, and the stock lost half its value one month after we purchased it. That loss taught us that we must do our homework before we purchase any stock—no matter who recommends it.

Your founding members must agree on the types of stocks in which your club will invest:

- *High-risk, speculative stocks,* which A. G. Edwards & Sons, Inc., defines as those stocks with above-average risk in terms of volatility and the possibility of significant loss
- *Medium-risk, aggressive stocks,* which are those stocks having uncertain future investment returns
- *Conservative, long-term growth stocks,* which are those stocks expected to grow at a rate greater than the general economy
- *A combination of all three*

An investment philosophy that has proven successful suggests investing in high-quality stocks with growth potential.

## 2. How Often Should You Invest?

Invest on a regular basis. Most likely your club will meet only once a month, so market timing—deciding the best time to invest—will be difficult. Successful investment clubs establish a definite schedule for purchasing stocks—not necessarily at every meeting, but on a regular basis—and they adhere to that schedule regardless of the market. My club makes a practice of purchasing stocks quarterly, although we make financial contributions every month. This allows us more time to accumulate money for our stock purchases. You will find more on investment schedules in Chapter 13.

### 3. What Should You Do with Your Earnings?

Reinvest your gains! This is a cardinal rule for successful long-term investing. To compound your wealth, reinvest the money you receive from dividends and the sale of securities. Don't use your gains to celebrate your accomplishments!

The primary goal of an investment club should be to learn how to invest. Of course, the more you know about investing, the better your investment decisions will be. And if you make sound, educated investment decisions, financial success surely will follow.

It's important that all members of your club, founding members and those who join later, understand and respect these ingredients of success. New members must make a time commitment to the club and they must feel comfortable with your club's investment philosophy, or disagreements may arise. It will soon become obvious (and unpleasant) if one member wants to invest only in speculative stocks, hoping to make a killing, while the rest of you are more comfortable investing in long-term growth stocks.

The first modern-day investment club and the forerunner to today's National Association of Investors Corporation (NAIC) began in Detroit in the 1940s. This early club developed an investment philosophy of investing on a regular schedule, investing in high-quality growth stocks and reinvesting all dividends and capital gains. By the early 1980s, each founding member of that club, having contributed $20 to $25 every month, had accumulated more than $200,000! Developed 50 years ago, this same in-

vestment philosophy continues to be the basis for successful investing today.

## Write a Mission Statement

After you've discussed the ingredients of a successful investment club and you all agree on the club's purpose, the
founding members should draft a mission statement, which
you should review periodically to make sure you stay on
track. The mission statement doesn't have to be fancy, it's
simply a written statement explaining the purpose and
goals of your club. This statement will prove very helpful if,
at sometime in the future, members have differences of
opinions regarding the club's direction. A simple statement
might say, for example, that the mission of your investment
club is to learn how to invest wisely in the stock market
without taking undue risk. To avoid my club's early stock di-
saster, you might also add that you will not purchase any
stock without first completing a thorough study of the
company whose stock you wish to buy. You'll be happy that
you have this statement to fall back on when one of your
members wants to buy a stock currently in vogue without
studying the numbers.

## Name Your Club

At the initial meeting, you also should decide on a name
for your club. The possibilities are endless. The teachers I
mentioned earlier call their club the Rockerfellas; another
club I know of is called the Gotstocks; and I am a member
of the Women's Investment Club. Name your club whatever
you'd like, so long as no other organization in your county
shares the same name. As a practical matter and before you
begin to work on the required legal documents outlined in
the next chapter, call or visit your county clerk's office to be

sure the name you've selected isn't already being used. One word of warning: Some newspapers make a practice of publishing new business registrations, including investment clubs and their members' names, so use discretion in naming your club.

The checklist in Figure 3.1 outlines the ingredients of success described in this chapter. It's important that all club members, both founding members and those who join later, understand and respect these ingredients to ensure the compatibility of all your club members.

**FIGURE 3.1**   Items To Discuss with Founding and New Members

# Ingredients of Success

## ✓ CHECKLIST

☐  1. Commitment

☐  2. Investment philosophy

    ☐  A. Long-term approach versus "get-rich-quick"

    ☐  B. Risk tolerance level
- Conservative
- Aggressive
- Speculative
- Combination of the above three

    ☐  C. Investment schedule

    ☐  D. Reinvest gains

☐  3. Mission statement

☐  4. Name for your club
(Check with county clerk for availability of name chosen.)

# Tips for Success

Don't Be Afraid To Seek Help

Take It One Step at a Time

Be Patient—Wall Street Wasn't Built in a Day

# CHAPTER 4

# STEP THREE:
## Conquering the Legal Requirements

$\mathcal{A}$ll businesses, including investment clubs, must fulfill certain legal and tax requirements before they can begin to purchase stocks. This chapter outlines the forms that are required and explains how to complete them. Your first decision will be what type of business structure your club will take. We'll discuss the pluses and minuses of the two types of structures available to you and which professionals can help you make the best decisions for your club.

## Possible Business Structures for Your Club

### Partnerships

Because of favorable tax treatment, most investment clubs have, until recently, chosen the partnership form of business structure. In a partnership, each partner shares in the ownership of the business, or in this case, the investment club. Partnerships themselves are not taxed by the Internal Revenue Service (IRS). Their profits or losses are passed on to each partner or club member, and each member has the responsibility to report his or her share of the club's profits on a personal tax return. Because the partnership itself is not taxed, favorable tax treatment results from having only one level of taxation (with each partner or member being taxed). In contrast, different types of corporations must pay a tax on their profits before passing them on to their shareholders (in the form of dividends), who also must pay a tax on the dividends they receive, resulting in two levels of taxation.

Unlike corporations that have a board of directors who oversee the business, all members or partners of an investment club partnership are responsible for decisions affecting the partnership. Unfortunately, partnership law has evolved to the point where, today, any partner can bind the entire partnership to a contractual obligation with an outside party regardless of what the partnership agreement may say to the contrary. For example, if someone offers one of your partners a hot deal on a "can't miss" stock and that partner accepts the offer on behalf of your investment club partnership, but without the club's authorization, your club is still legally bound by the partner's acceptance.

Assuming your founding members are friends and coworkers, you probably feel that you have no reason to be concerned about a member's ability to bind the club. I hope you're right. But the old saying still rings true: "An ounce of prevention is worth a pound of cure."

## Voluntary Cooperative Associations

To avoid possible future difficulties, you can explore a new and innovative approach: Your proposed investment club can become a voluntary cooperative association. A cooperative association is simply a group of people who band together to further a common purpose or business. Since the IRS has not yet developed specific requirements for cooperative associations, it will treat your club as a corporation or a partnership, depending on the way your club operates. Thus, if your club becomes a cooperative association with its characteristics most closely resembling a partnership (making business decisions as a group), it will be subject to the same tax requirements as a partnership. In other words, the law will treat your club as a cooperative association, while the IRS will treat it as a partnership in which individual members are taxed, but not the club itself.

The most compelling reason for your club to consider the cooperative association approach is that individual members of a cooperative association cannot bind the entire association. Only the club's duly authorized officers can do this. In other words, an association would be bound by an agreement only if an authorized officer made the agreement. Your club's operating rules, described later in this chapter, outline club authority and responsibility. Authorized officers, however, are the president, vice president, secretary and treasurer elected by your membership. Their terms of office also are determined by your membership, but as a rule, officers should not hold the same office for more than two years. Each officer's responsibilities are outlined in Chapter 5.

## Which Professionals Can Help Your Club

### *An Attorney*

Meet with an attorney of corporate law first to decide which form of business structure your club will take. *Note:* Local laws regulating investment clubs vary from state to state.

### *An Accountant*

Next, discuss the tax implications of your club's chosen business structure with an accountant. Remember: If your club becomes a voluntary cooperative association and the club's characteristics most closely resemble the criteria established for partnerships, you'll be treated as a partnership for tax purposes. So the IRS will not tax your club, but it will allow your club to pass its gains or losses on to each member, who must then report them on his or her individual tax return.

Recently, there have been instances where the IRS has taxed investment club associations as corporations rather than as partnerships. To date, the IRS Code has not changed; there is no law stating that associations should be taxed the same as corporations are taxed. The Code, however, is subject to individual interpretation, and for this reason it is imperative that you seek the advice of an accountant before you file the necessary legal documents for your club's business structure.

You may be hesitant to seek the advice of an attorney and an accountant because of the professional fees you will incur. But it's important that you make these contacts now to lay the groundwork for your club's future needs; it's not fair to wait until late February or early March, the busiest time of the year for these professionals, to introduce yourself and expect them to respond quickly to your needs. In Chapter 5 you can find the tasks you must complete to get your club off and running.

## Filing Income Tax Returns

The IRS requires all business entities, whether they are partnerships or cooperative associations, to file an annual return. Since the IRS hasn't developed a specific return for cooperative associations, your treasurer, with an accountant's help, will have to file an annual partnership return (Form 1065) even if your club's business structure takes the association approach. Additionally, at the end of the year, your club's treasurer must provide each member with a Schedule K-1, a report of his or her profits or losses for the year, which each member must declare on his or her personal tax return.

The IRS has given investment clubs special consideration, however. It allows clubs to file a one-time annual partnership return with an accompanying statement identifying each founding club member and declaring that the club qualifies as an investment club partnership (even if, legally, you're considered an association). Your treasurer should ask your club's accountant to draft this statement for you. After filing your one-time partnership return and accompanying statement with the IRS, your club will not have to file a partnership return in future years. This holds true even if your club's membership changes.

Although your club won't have to file a partnership return after its first year if it meets IRS requirements, your treasurer must continue to furnish each member of your club with a statement of his or her profits or losses for the year to be reported on a personal tax return. Again, an accountant can help your treasurer prepare this annual information and inform your treasurer whether the tax rules for investment clubs have changed during the year.

## Sorting Out the Paperwork

After you've decided your proposed club's business structure, you must fulfill certain legal conditions for the structure you select. Following is an outline of these conditions. These requirements are shown in diagram form in Figure 4.1.

**FIGURE 4.1**    Legal Requirements for Starting an Investment Club

All businesses, including investment clubs, must register as a legal entity to satisfy the Internal Revenue Service. You may choose either of the following structures, but you should consult an attorney and an accountant to ensure that you meet state regulations. An attorney also should review your articles of association or partnership agreement.

### Voluntary Cooperative Association

Individual members of an association cannot bind the entire association. Only duly authorized officers can do this.

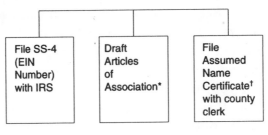

### Partnerships

Individual members of a general partnership can bind the entire partnership to a contractual obligation with an outside party, regardless of what the partnership agreement may say to the contrary.

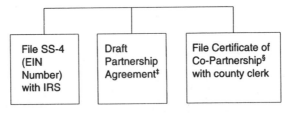

*See sample in Appendix A.
†See sample in Figure 4.3.
‡See sample in Appendix B.
§See sample in Figure 4.4.

### *Obtaining an Employer Identification Number*

After you've met with an attorney and an accountant to discuss the legal and tax consequences of starting an investment club, you should file for an employer identification number (EIN). To secure your number, you must complete the IRS's application, Form SS-4. Figure 4.2 shows a sample form, which is available at your local IRS office. Every business, including investment clubs, must have this identification number, which your club's broker and the IRS will use to identify your club's account. When completing the EIN application, you'll need to identify your investment club by name and specify one member, usually your club's treasurer, to act as the contact person.

### *Establishing Operating Rules*

Your next step is to draw up a set of rules or guidelines that describe how your club will operate. Bylaws are the operating rules of a corporation. If your club decides to become a cooperative association, it must adopt Articles of Association, the document that specifies how your association will operate. If, on the other hand, your club elects to become a partnership, your club must adopt what is called a Partnership Agreement, the document that outlines the partnership's rules of operation. You will find samples of both documents in the Appendix. Depending on the business structure you choose, ask your attorney to review the appropriate document to ensure that it meets your state's regulations. You also may want to amend this instrument to meet your club's particular needs. Before each member signs the document, however, be sure that he or she has carefully read it and agrees to abide by these rules.

Your club should amend the Partnership Agreement whenever a change in your membership occurs. In my club, we've found it very difficult to secure every member's signature on an amended agreement whenever we take in a new partner or lose a partner, so we've made a practice of

**FIGURE 4.2**  Sample IRS Form SS-4

| Form **SS-4**<br>(Rev. December 1993)<br>Department of the Treasury<br>Internal Revenue Service | **Application for Employer Identification Number**<br>(For use by employers, corporations, partnerships, trusts, estates, churches, government agencies, certain individuals, and others. **See instructions.**) | EIN |
|---|---|---|
| | | OMB No. 1545-0003<br>Expires 12-31-96 |

Please type or print clearly.

**1** Name of applicant (Legal name) (See instructions.)
INVESTMENT CLUB'S NAME

**2** Trade name of business, if different from name in line 1

**3** Executor, trustee, "care of" name
NAME OF MEMBER TO CONTACT

**4a** Mailing address (street address) (room, apt., or suite no.)
CONTACT'S ADDRESS

**4b** City, state, and ZIP code

**5a** Business address, if different from address in lines 4a and 4b

**5b** City, state, and ZIP code

**6** County and state where principal business is located

**7** Name of principal officer, general partner, grantor, owner, or trustor—SSN required (See instructions.) ▶

**8a** Type of entity (Check only one box.) (See instructions.)
☐ Sole Proprietor (SSN)
☐ REMIC   ☐ Personal service corp.
☐ State/local government   ☐ National guard
☐ Other nonprofit organization (specify)
☒ Other (specify) ▶ STATE WHETHER VOLUNTARY COOPERATIVE ASSN. OR PARTNERSHIP

☐ Estate (SSN of decedent)
☐ Plan administrator-SSN
☐ Other corporation (specify)
☐ Federal government/military   ☐ Church or church controlled organization
(enter GEN if applicable)

☐ Trust
☐ Partnership
☐ Farmers' cooperative

**8b** If a corporation, name the state or foreign country
(if applicable) where incorporated ▶

| State | Foreign country |
|---|---|
| | |

**9** Reason for applying (Check only one box.)

☒ Started new business (specify) ▶ investment club
☐ Hired employees
☐ Created a pension plan (specify type) ▶
☐ Banking purpose (specify) ▶
☐ Changed type of organization (specify) ▶
☐ Purchased going business
☐ Created a trust (specify) ▶
☐ Other (specify) ▶

**10** Date business started or acquired (Mo., day, year) (See instructions.)

**11** Enter closing month of accounting year. (See instructions.)

**12** First date wages or annuities were paid or will be paid (Mo., day, year). **Note:** *If applicant is a withholding agent, enter date income will first be paid to nonresident alien. (Mo., day, year)* ▶

**13** Enter highest number of employees expected in the next 12 months. **Note:** *If the applicant does not expect to have any employees during the period, enter "0."*

| Nonagricultural | Agricultural | Household |
|---|---|---|
| | | |

**14** Principal activity (See instructions.) ▶ INVESTMENT CLUB

**15** Is the principal business activity manufacturing? . . . . . . . . . . ☐ Yes ☒ No
If "Yes," principal product and raw material used ▶

**16** To whom are most of the products or services sold?  Please check the appropriate box.   ☐ Business (wholesale)   ☒ N/A
☐ Public (retail)   ☐ Other (specify) ▶

**17a** Has the applicant ever applied for an identification number for this or any other business? . . . . . ☐ Yes ☒ No
**Note:** *If "Yes," please complete lines 17b and 17c.*

**17b** If you checked the "Yes" box in line 17a, give applicant's legal name and trade name, if different than name shown on prior application.

Legal name ▶                                        Trade name ▶

**17c** Enter approximate date, city, and state where the application was filed and the previous employer identification number if known.

| Approximate date when filed (Mo., day, year) | City and state where filed | Previous EIN |
|---|---|---|
| | | |

Under penalties of perjury, I declare that I have examined this application, and to the best of my knowledge and belief, it is true, correct, and complete.   Business telephone number (include area code)

Name and title (Please type or print clearly.) ▶ (EITHER PRESIDENT or TREASURER)

Signature ▶ (WHOEVER IS THE CONTACT PERSON)                          Date ▶

**Note:** *Do not write below this line.*   *For official use only.*

| Please leave blank ▶ | Geo. | Ind. | Class | Size | Reason for applying |
|---|---|---|---|---|---|
| | | | | | |

**For Paperwork Reduction Act Notice, see attached instructions.**   Cat. No. 16055N   Form **SS-4** (Rev. 12-93)

asking each new member to sign a simple statement saying that she has read our club's Partnership Agreement and agrees to abide by the rules of operation as outlined in that document. Then, at our first meeting of the new year, we pass around an amended Partnership Agreement and ask each member to sign the revised document. If your club elects to become a voluntary cooperative association, you do not need to amend your Articles of Association whenever your membership changes.

### *Protecting Your Club's Name*

Two documents can protect the name you choose for your investment club. Once you have registered the appropriate document with the county clerk, your club's name cannot be used by any other business in that county.

1.  If your club takes the cooperative association form of business structure, you must complete a certificate of persons conducting business under assumed name (more commonly referred to as a "DBA"—doing business as).
2.  If, however, your club becomes a partnership, you need to complete a certificate of co-partnership.

You can obtain these forms from your county clerk, and you will have to pay a nominal registration fee when filing either of these documents. Figure 4.3 shows you the State of Michigan's certificate of persons conducting business under assumed name. Figure 4.4 is a copy of Michigan's certificate of co-partnership. Both of these forms remain in effect for a specified number of years. Your county clerk should notify you when it is time to renew the document, and each member will have to sign the updated certificate. Again, if your club becomes a partnership, you will have to amend your certificate of co-partnership whenever a change in your membership occurs. Ask your county clerk, however, if you will have to update your certificate of persons conducting business under assumed name every time your membership changes. Both documents, the DBA and certificate of co-partnership, are state documents and may vary somewhat from state to state.

The checklist in Figure 4.5 itemizes the specific requirements you must fulfill before your club can begin operating and whom you should contact to accomplish each of these prerequisites.

## You're in Business!

Finally! You've satisfied the legal and tax requirements to become an investment club. You've met with an attorney and an accountant and, with their help, decided whether to become a cooperative association or a partnership. You've secured an employer identification number from the IRS, you've drafted your rules of operation, and you've filed the necessary document to register your club's name. Your investment club is now a business. Congratulations!

**FIGURE 4.3** Sample Certificate of Persons Conducting Business Under Assumed Name

𝔠𝔢𝔯𝔱𝔦𝔣𝔦𝔠𝔞𝔱𝔢 𝔬𝔣 ℌ𝔢𝔯𝔰𝔬𝔫𝔰 𝔠𝔬𝔫𝔡𝔲𝔠𝔱𝔦𝔫𝔤 𝔅𝔲𝔰𝔦𝔫𝔢𝔰𝔰 𝔘𝔫𝔡𝔢𝔯 𝔄𝔰𝔰𝔲𝔪𝔢𝔡 𝔑𝔞𝔪𝔢

STATE OF MICHIGAN, } ss.
COUNTY OF GRAND TRAVERSE }                    FILING FEE $10.00

The undersigned certifies that they now own or intend to own, conduct or transact business at:

Street Address __Address of Contact Person.__

City/State/Zip _____.

Grand Traverse County, Michigan under the assumed name of __
__Name of Investment Club.__

The undersigned further certifies that the true or real full name and the address of the person[1] owning, conducting or transacting said business is:

**PRINT OR TYPE NAMES AND ADDRESS**

NAME              STREET ADDRESS              CITY/STATE/ZIP

__List Founding Members.__
_____  _____  _____
_____  _____  _____
_____  _____  _____
_____  _____  _____

***In Witness Whereof,*** I/We have this date of _____ 19_____. made and signed this certificate

**SIGNATURES OF PERSONS CONDUCTING BUSINESS UNDER ASSUMED NAME**

__All Members must sign in front__
__of notary.__
_____  _____
_____  _____

## STATE OF MICHIGAN, } ss.
COUNTY OF GRAND TRAVERSE

On_____, 19___, before me, a Notary Public, personally appeared the above named person or persons, whose signatures appear above, and who executed the foregoing instrument, and ___he___ acknowledged to me that ___he___ executed the same, and that they are all of the persons now owning, conducting and transacting or who intend to own, conduct and transact the business under the above name.

Notary Public, _____ County, Michigan

My commission expires _____ 19___

**THIS CERTIFICATE EXPIRES FIVE YEARS FROM DATE OF FILING WITH COUNTY CLERK**

*This portion to be filled in only by the County Clerk*

**THIS CERTIFICATE EXPIRES** _____

## STATE OF MICHIGAN, } ss.
COUNTY OF GRAND TRAVERSE

I, Virginia A. Watson, Clerk of the County aforesaid and Clerk of the Circuit Court for said County, do hereby certify that I have compared the within copy of Certificate setting forth the full names of the persons owning, conducting or transacting business under the name of_____

together with the certificate of filing endorsed thereon, with the original Certificate heretofore filed and now remaining in my office, and that it is a true and correct copy thereof, and of the whole of such original Certificate and of said certificate of filing.

***In Testimony Whereof,*** I have hereunto set my hand and affixed the seal of said Circuit Court, on _____, 19___.

Virginia A. Watson

_____ County Clerk

By _____

NOTE: This Certificate must be renewed within five (5) years from date. If you change your place of business you must notify this office. If you change the personnel above listed you must file Notice of Dissolution and a new Certificate with this office. If you discontinue your business you must file Notice of Dissolution with this office.

1. "Person" may be one or more individuals, corporations, partnerships, limited partnerships, trusts, fiduciaries or other entity. In case of a person other than an individual, see MSA 19.826 (MCL 445.4) for details to be stated in certificate.

**FIGURE 4.4**    Sample Certificate of Co-Partnership

*Certificate of Co-Partnership*

STATE OF MICHIGAN, } ss.
COUNTY OF GRAND TRAVERSE

FILING FEE $10.00

**THIS CERTIFIES THAT** we, whose names are signed hereunder in full, are joined in co-partnership

under the firm name of ____Name of Investment Club_____
(Write on this line the full name of your firm)

located at ____Address of Contact Person_____, State of Michigan.
(Give name of town on this line and if you are located in a city or village having street numbers, give your street and number)

**PRINT OR TYPE NAMES AND ADDRESSES OF CO-PARTNERS**

| NAME | STREET ADDRESS | CITY OR TOWN |
|------|----------------|--------------|
| List Founding Members | | |
| | | |
| | | |
| | | |
| | | |

**In Witness Whereof,** We have this _____ day of _____

19____, made and signed this certificate

**This Certificate Expires Five (5) Years from the date of filing with the County Clerk.**

**SIGNATURES OF CO-PARTNERS**

All Partners Must Sign.

| | |
|--|--|
| | |
| | |

## STATE OF MICHIGAN,
## COUNTY OF GRAND TRAVERSE } ss.

I, _____

one of the co-partners of the said firm of _____
(Write in name of firm on this line)

do hereby certify that all co-partners of said firm have herein above individually subscribed their respective names as witnessed by myself, and that the place of residence of each said co-partner as above written is true and correct.

(Signed) **X** ____Only 1 Partner Must Sign in Front of Notary.____
(One of the co-partners of above named firm)

Subscribed and Sworn to before me this _____ day of _____ 19_____

Notary Public, _____ County, Michigan

My commission expires _____ 19_____

Virginia A. Watson

## STATE OF MICHIGAN,
## COUNTY OF GRAND TRAVERSE } ss.

I, _____ Clerk of the County aforesaid and Clerk of the Circuit Court for said County, do hereby certify that I have compared the within copy of Certificate setting forth the full names of the persons owning, conducting or transacting business under the name of _____

together with the certificate of filing endorsed thereon, with the original Certificate heretofore filed and now remaining in my office, and that it is a true and correct copy thereof, and of the whole of such original Certificate and of said certificate of filing.

**In Testimony Whereof,** I have hereunto set my hand and affixed the seal of said Circuit Court, this _____ day of _____ 19_____.

Virginia A. Watson

[SEAL]

By _____ County Clerk

**FIGURE 4.5**    Legal Requirements Checklist

# Legal Requirements

---

## ✓ CHECKLIST

| Item | Contact |
|------|---------|
| ☐  Decide legal structure (cooperative association or partnership) and determine the tax consequences. | Attorney and accountant |
| ☐  Draft articles of association or partnership agreement. All members must review and sign appropriate document. | Attorney should review |
| ☐  File Form SS-4 (EIN number). Designate one member to act as contact person. | Accountant or local IRS office |
| ☐  File assumed name certificate or certificate of copartnership. All members must sign appropriate document. | County clerk |

# Tips for Success

Take Yourselves Seriously

Operate Your Club as a Business

Organize, Organize, Organize

# CHAPTER 5

# STEP FOUR:
## Setting Up a Winning Club

*M*any articles on investment clubs suggest they also become social gatherings, meeting at members' homes for coffee or dessert. My club tried this approach: We spent our first three years meeting at dining room tables or on outdoor decks. After our meetings, we knew about every social event that had taken place during the past month, but we didn't gain much investment knowledge. When we finally took stock, so to speak, we found our club's portfolio was down 29 percent—this in a bull market. Something was obviously wrong!

Investment clubs often fail because members don't take themselves or their goals seriously. You will have many decisions to make, and it may take several meetings to accomplish what your club needs to do to be successful. This chapter outlines all the structural decisions you must make so your club can operate effectively. You can use the checklist in Figure 5.1 to help you track your progress.

## Steps in Building a Successful Club

### 1. Set a Date for Your Monthly Meetings

Be specific: Select, for example, the third Monday of each month, and stick to that date. If you start changing meeting dates, you'll spend valuable meeting time comparing each other's calendars.

### 2. Set a Place for Your Monthly Meetings

You'll be more efficient and take yourselves more seriously in a business-like setting, such as a conference room, member's office or schoolroom. If you meet around the kitchen table, you invite food, family, phone and other interruptions.

### 3. Set a Time To Meet and a Time To Adjourn

Meetings that last indefinitely accomplish less than those with a predetermined time limit, and you risk losing your members' attention. My club now meets at 5:00 P.M., and we adjourn no later than 7:00 P.M., often earlier. We save socializing for after our meetings.

### 4. Decide on an Amount Each Member Must Contribute Monthly for Investment Purposes

There's no rule for contributions; the amount should be whatever your members can comfortably afford. My club's 20 members contribute $25 a month—that's $6,000 annually! Other clubs set their contributions rate considerably higher, and some require a one-time or once-a-year contribution of $500 to $1,000. Again, investment clubs come in all sizes and shapes. As soon as you begin making financial contributions to your club, though, make sure that one member keeps a record of everyone's payments.

## 5. *Elect Officers To Fulfill the Responsibilities Indicated*

The following is a list of corporate titles your club should use if it is a voluntary cooperative association. Officers of partnerships, however, are referred to as presiding partners, recording partners and the like; these titles are also shown. As a rule, officers should not hold the same office for more than two years; they tend to lose their enthusiasm. When your membership is small, however, it will be difficult to elect new officers every year. But as your membership grows, you'll have more members who are able to serve.

A. President/Presiding partner
  (Must have good organizational skills.)
  - Conducts meetings.
  - Formulates the monthly agenda.
B. Vice president/Assisting presiding partner
  (Must have good organizational skills and be able to assist president.)
  - Conducts meetings in president's absence.
  - Assists president when necessary.
C. Secretary/Recording partner
  (Must possess good writing skills.)
  - Takes notes and prepares minutes of formal meetings.
  - Handles necessary correspondence.
D. Treasurer/Financial partner
  (Should have access to a computer spreadsheet program.)
  - Prepares a monthly financial report (see Figure 8.1).
  - Prepares year-end tax information.

- Liaison between club and club's broker.
- Places buy/sell orders with broker.
E.  Assistant treasurer/Assisting financial partner
    (Should be comfortable working with numbers and
    have knowledge of the spreadsheet program the
    treasurer uses.)
    - Assists treasurer.
    - Handles club's checking account.

## 6. Send Meeting Notices or Reminders One Week in Advance

Our club uses our forthcoming meeting's agenda as a reminder, and we also include a copy of the previous month's
minutes in this mailing. Our president drafts each month's
agenda, and gives it to our secretary, who types it and mails
it with the minutes. If your secretary doesn't handle your
mailings, be sure the member designated to do this has
access to a typewriter or word processor and a copy machine. Tips for developing an agenda are presented in
Chapter 6.

## 7. Open a Checking Account To Pay Administrative Expenses

These expenses include postage, copy paper and enve-
lopes for mailing meeting notices. If, in January, we find
that our bank balance is low, each member of my club pays
an additional $25 to cover these expenses for the year. Be-
cause you'll have initial start-up costs such as accountant
and attorney fees and your assumed name certificate or certificate of copartnership registration fees, you'll probably
need to contribute more than $25 when you first open your
checking account. But wait until you know your start-up expenses before deciding how much to contribute. Remember, this checking account contribution is in addition
to your monthly investment contributions.

When you open your checking account, you'll also have to decide who will have authority to sign checks. Obviously, your assistant treasurer should sign if he or she is in charge of the checkbook, but I recommend requiring two signatures on all the checks you write. If you make this a requirement, you'll need to give a third club member authority to sign checks in the absence of one of your two authorized signers.

## 8. Select a Stockbroker

This individual should be asked to share investment knowledge, offer useful resource materials and provide the necessary financial services your club will need. Most beginning investment clubs use a broker, and you'll find it helpful to be able to call upon your broker to answer your investment questions. You can choose a broker who is already handling a member's personal transactions or a broker who has been recommended to you. Stockbrokers new to the brokerage business may value the opportunity to serve your club in the hope of becoming better known. Take time to interview potential brokers; you can appoint two members of your club to do this and make recommendations to the club. Here are some questions you should ask potential brokers:

- *What are the commission fees?* These fees are the amount of money the brokerage firm will charge your club every time you buy or sell stocks. Be sure you understand how these fees are determined, and ask the broker you select to provide you with a rate schedule.
- *Does the brokerage firm have a seat on the New York Stock Exchange, the American Stock Exchange and all other major exchanges?*
- *Is the brokerage firm covered by the Securities Investor Protection Corporation (SIPC)?* This is similar to FDIC insurance coverage for banks; it won't

protect you from falling stock prices, but it will
protect against improprieties.

- *What is the broker's investment philosophy?* Be
  certain that the broker has a philosophy that is com-
  patible with that of your club.
- *Will the broker allow club members to use the brokerage firm's resource materials?* These materials include *Value Line's* and *Standard & Poor's* reports,
  discussed in Chapter 12. You may want to visit the
  broker's office and make copies yourself or request a
  fax directly from Standard & Poor's.

### 9. *Open a Brokerage Account with Your Broker's Firm*

Most firms require that each member of the investment
club sign a fairly standardized agreement with the brokerage firm before an account can be opened. A. G. Edwards & Sons, Inc., calls their agreement an Investment
Club Account Agreement, and its primary purpose is to
name the club member or members who have the authority
to buy and sell stocks on the investment club's behalf. This
agreement also discusses liability and arbitration in case of
litigation. If your club takes the partnership form of
business structure, update these forms whenever your
club's membership changes. If your club becomes a voluntary association, it may not be necessary to update the
brokerage firm agreement when a change in your membership occurs, but you should discuss this with your
broker to be sure of the firm's requirements.

### 10. *Open a Money Market Account with Your Broker's Firm*

Deposit your monthly investment contributions to earn
interest while you research stocks to purchase. If your club
doesn't have enough money available to open such an ac-

count, deposit your monthly contributions in your club's checking account until you have accumulated the necessary funds. Otherwise, each member can make a substantial one-time contribution to meet the financial requirements of opening this money market account.

## 11. *Contact the NAIC*

The National Association of Investors Corporation (NAIC) (P.O. Box 220, Royal Oak, Michigan 48068; 810-583-6242) is an organization that provides its members with a means to broaden their investment interest and investment knowledge. To serve this purpose, the NAIC offers its members a number of benefits:

- Investment and accounting seminars
- A stock study course
- Stock study guides
- Workshops and videos explaining how to complete and add judgment to the study guides
- A low-cost investment plan
- An accounting kit
- Subscription to the magazine *Better Investing*. However, you need not be a member of the NAIC to subscribe to its investment magazine.

The NAIC charges each member investment club a low annual fee. Each club member is also assessed an additional small annual fee. Belonging to the NAIC does not mean that you belong to two investment clubs, but it enables your club to use the services offered by this organization.

# What Comes Next?

You've fulfilled the steps required to form and organize your investment club. The difficult part is over. Part 2 addresses the month-to-month operations of your club.

Chapter 7 describes the unit accounting system; this accounting system will begin to make sense as you work with it. Chapter 11 suggests ways to expand your club's horizon after your club has been operating for a year or more.

---

**FIGURE 5.1** Club Structure Checklist

# Club Structure

## ✓ CHECKLIST

☐ 1. Date of monthly meetings: _____

☐ 2. Location of meetings: _____

☐ 3. Time of meetings: _____

☐ 4. Amount of monthly investment contributions: _____

☐ 5. Officers:

    ☐ A. President/Presiding partner

    ☐ B. Vice president/Assisting presiding partner

    ☐ C. Secretary/Recording partner

    ☐ D. Treasurer/Financial partner

    ☐ E. Assistant treasurer/Assisting financial partner

☐ 6. Appoint one member to handle mailings: _____

**FIGURE 5.1**   Club Structure Checklist  (Continued)

☐   7.  Open checking account.

    ☐   A.  Amount needed to open account: $ _____

    ☐   B.  Appoint three members to sign checks:
        1. _____
        2. _____
        3. _____

☐   8.  Select a stockbroker: _____

    ☐   A.  Must be willing to share knowledge.

    ☐   B.  Must have a similar investment philosophy.

    ☐   C.  Must allow members to use firm's resources.

    ☐   D.  Should provide a commission rate schedule.

    ☐   E.  Brokerage firm should be a member of all major exchanges.

    ☐   F.  Brokerage firm should have insurance coverage against improprieties.

☐   9.  Complete brokerage firm's agreements, if required.

☐   10.  Open a money market account as soon as club has necessary funds.

☐   11.  Contact NAIC for introductory packet of materials.

# Part Two

# OPERATING FOR SUCCESS

Challenges can be stepping stones or
stumbling blocks. It's just a matter of how
you view them.

*Anonymous*

# Tips for Success

Be Flexible

Encourage Discussion

Report on All Stocks in Club's Portfolio

CHAPTER 6

# DEVELOPING AN AGENDA THAT KEEPS YOU ON TRACK

$\mathcal{T}$he meetings of your investment club must be structured in such a way as to ensure your time is well spent. The best tool for conducting organized meetings is an agenda. One week prior to our upcoming meeting, we send each member the agenda of our forthcoming meeting along with the minutes of our previous meeting. This mailing serves two purposes: It reminds our members of the following week's meeting, and it gives members time to review the minutes before the next meeting.

The sample agenda illustrated in Figure 6.1 includes many items your club can use to conduct meaningful, successful meetings. The subjects under items I and II of the figure are self-explanatory. Item III, "$ contribution for investment purposes," is included as a reminder to your members to submit their checks to your treasurer. In item IV, your club's treasurer will furnish facts and figures re-

**FIGURE 6.1**   Sample Agenda

(Date of Meeting)
(Time and Place of Meeting)
**A G E N D A**

I.  Call to order

II.  Acceptance of minutes of (date of previous meeting)

III.  $_____contribution for investment purposes

IV.  Financial report—treasurer

V.  Portfolio
   A.  Old business
      1.  Current holdings
         a.  Comments by members responsible
            i.  XYZ Co.
            ii.  SAIL
            iii.  BBB Corp.
         b.  Other
      2.  Other old business
   B.  New business
      1.  Prospective purchases
         a.  Report by (beverage industry)
         b.  Other stock presentations
      2.  Investment Decisions

VI.  Education: Annual reports by Diane and Alice

VII.  Items for next month's meeting
   A.  Industry to be presented
   B.  Educational topic
   C.  Time and place of next meeting

VIII.  Adjournment

lating to your club's investment performance and your ownership value. This will be explained further in subsequent chapters. Item V is devoted to your club's portfolio: its current holdings and prospective purchases. This is the time when you should hear a report on each of the stocks your club owns. Do you know of any specific news that may affect the company's earnings? Is an updated *Value Line* report available on the company? These are the types of questions that should be asked. Later, you may have comments to make on previously held stocks, or you may want to continue a discussion held over from last month's meeting. Under item V, the beverage industry is used merely as an example. Also, as I recommend in my discussion on taking the industry approach to investing in Chapter 12, encourage your members to present stocks they've been following on their own at this point in the meeting. Be sure to bring a newspaper with the previous day's stock quotations to your meetings so you'll have current prices for the stocks in your portfolio and those you're analyzing for purchase.

If you decide to devote a portion of your meetings to education, include the topic to be discussed as a separate agenda item. In the figure, "annual reports" is the subject to be presented.

This sample agenda is deliberately very detailed so that it's easy to understand; certainly you can revise it to meet your club's needs. Indeed, you'll find that, since your president will draft each month's agenda, it is likely the format will change whenever you have a new president. Your agenda also will differ if your meeting structure changes, such as when you have a guest speaker address your club. Otherwise, you will find that the format for your agenda will remain about the same from month to month.

There is no way to decide how much time you should devote to each section of the agenda. If you send out the previous month's minutes before the meeting, you shouldn't have to spend meeting time reviewing them before acceptance. The major portion of your meetings should be spent hearing reports on the stocks you own, the stocks you are considering for purchase and education. Your president has responsibility for keeping the meetings moving, and that is why you need a president who has strong leadership skills. As your club evolves, you'll have other or different items to add to your agenda. Regardless of format or other cosmetic differences, however, it is important that your agenda contain a basic list of the items you want to address at each meeting. Also, especially in the early stages of your meetings, *keep it simple.* Most of your members will be beginning investors, and they will want to concentrate on their objective of learning how to invest in the stock market through the buying and selling of securities. They should not get bogged down in the details of organization.

Meeting structure is important, but your president must allow time for general discussion. Perhaps a club member has brought copies of an investment article to share with the membership. Or maybe a member has recently read a book of interest that he or she would like to discuss. Through your investment discussions you may discover an investment topic you don't fully understand. This, in turn, may lead to a discussion of speakers who could address your club on that topic. Your president should encourage exchange to generate ideas and share knowledge.

# Tips for Success

Review the System until You Understand It

Make Timely Contributions

CHAPTER 7

# CREATING AN ACCOUNTING SYSTEM EVERYONE CAN UNDERSTAND

𝒪nce your club begins to purchase stock, you must be able to determine the value of the club's portfolio and each member's share in that value. This way you'll be able to gauge how well your investments are performing and whether you and your club are making money. At each monthly meeting, your treasurer will prepare and distribute to each club member a financial report, explained in Chapter 8, that includes this information. Chapter 7 is a building block for Chapter 8. It will show you how to place a value on one share of your investment club. You will then learn how to determine how many shares in your club your monthly contribution will purchase and finally how to calculate the value of the total number of shares you own—your individual net value.

## Determining Membership Value—The Unit Accounting System

The unit accounting system will help you determine each member's individual net value in the club. First, we'll explain how to determine the number of units in the club. Next we'll show you how to place a value on one unit or share in the club. Then you'll learn how to determine the number of units your monthly contributions will buy. Finally, we'll be able to calculate membership value—the total dollar amount your units are worth. Because this system is a little complex, you can use the examples to help you work through the explanation of the unit accounting system. For easy reference, Figure 7.1 illustrates Part IV of the monthly financial report; it is a sample of the unit accounting system at work. Figure 7.2 summarizes this method of determining unit and membership values. These are the building blocks of the financial reports.

### *Buying Club Units or Shares*

Think of your investment club as a company in which each member owns shares of stock or units. Every time you make a monthly investment contribution, that contribution is deposited into your club's money market account to await your stock purchase decisions. Your contribution also is used to purchase shares or units in the club itself.

As a starting point, let's assume that your club's monthly investment contributions have been set at $25. Now, assign a dollar value to one unit—say one unit is worth $25—and assume that each member has contributed a total of $250 (monthly contributions of $25 × 10 months). Thus, after 10 months, each member owns 10 units of your club, as shown below.

$250 Total contributions to date
÷ $25 Amount of monthly contributions
= 10.000 Ownership units

**FIGURE 7.1**   Sample of Part IV of Financial Report

**PART IV: Membership Value**

Portfolio Value: $2,100.00

Portfolio value/total base units = $ value per unit

($2,100 ÷ 80.000 = $26.25 per unit)

New individual contribution/$ value per unit = new units

($25 contribution ÷ $26.25 = 0.925 unit)

| Name | Total Contributions | Base Units | New Units | Total Units | % Club Owned | Market Value/ Units | Individual Net | Individual Gain/Loss | % Individual Gain/Loss |
|---|---|---|---|---|---|---|---|---|---|
| Susan | $ 275.00 | 10.000 | 0.952 | 10.952 | 12.50 | $26.25 | $ 287.49 | $12.49 | 4.54 |
| Alice | $ 275.00 | 10.000 | 0.952 | 10.952 | 12.50 | $26.25 | $ 287.49 | $12.49 | 4.54 |
| Mary | $ 275.00 | 10.000 | 0.952 | 10.952 | 12.50 | $26.25 | $ 287.49 | $12.49 | 4.54 |
| Ann | $ 275.00 | 10.000 | 0.952 | 10.952 | 12.50 | $26.25 | $ 287.49 | $12.49 | 4.54 |
| Nancy | $ 275.00 | 10.000 | 0.952 | 10.952 | 12.50 | $26.25 | $ 287.49 | $12.49 | 4.54 |
| Diane | $ 275.00 | 10.000 | 0.952 | 10.952 | 12.50 | $26.25 | $ 287.49 | $12.49 | 4.54 |
| Jean | $ 275.00 | 10.000 | 0.952 | 10.952 | 12.50 | $26.25 | $ 287.49 | $12.49 | 4.54 |
| Carol | $ 275.00 | 10.000 | 0.952 | 10.952 | 12.50 | $26.25 | $ 287.49 | $12.49 | 4.54 |
| **Total** | **$2,200.00** | **80.000** | **7.616** | **87.616** | **100.00** | | **$2,299.92** | **$99.92** | |

**FIGURE 7.2** Determining Unit and Membership Values

---

### Determining Unit Value

1. *Determine base value*
   $25 = 1 Unit
   Each member paid to date: $250
   $250 ÷ $25 = 10.000 units per member
   10.000 units × 8 members = 80.000 total club units

2. *Determine monthly portfolio value*
   Value of current stocks owned plus cash in money market
   account per most current statement received from your
   brokerage firm. (Do not include cash collected at current meeting
   or money in checking account.)
   Assume portfolio value = $2,100

3. *Determine current value*
   (Unit value determines number of units your monthly investment
   contribution will purchase each month.)
   Divide portfolio value by total club units:
   $2,100 ÷ 80.000 = $26.25

4. *Determine amount of new units purchased by members*
   Divide monthly investment contribution by current month's unit
   value:
   $25 ÷ $26.25 = 0.952

---

This example shows you how to begin calculating unit value. You won't need to determine how many units are owned in the club for the first few months you are in operation, because you'll be busy getting your club organized. Start this accounting system when you begin to invest in the stock market.

**FIGURE 7.2**    (Continued)

### Determining Membership Value

1. Determine total units owned by each member by adding current month's units to last month's units:
   10.000 units + 0.952 = 10.952 units

2. Determine new monthly total units for club by multiplying the total units per person by the number of members:
   10.952 units × 8 members = 87.616 club units

*Note:* If members have differing units of ownership, you cannot multiply the total units per person by the number of members in your club. Rather, you must *add* each member's total units to determine the total number of units owned in your club.

3. For following month, determine portfolio value, then use new total club unit figure of 87.616 as the base unit total.

4. To determine percent ownership, divide individual member's units by total club units:
   10.952 units ÷ 87.616 club units = 12.50%

Notice that Figure 7.1 shows a portfolio value of $2,100. This is the value of the $2,000 beginning contributions that you have invested in the stock market. Even though your club's contributions now total $2,200, according to Figure 7.1 your calculations to determine unit value are based on the amount of contributions that you have invested. This information is taken directly from your brokerage firm's monthly statement to your club. There will be a time lapse between the time you give your monthly contribution to your treasurer and the time these monies actually appear on the monthly financial statement provided by your brokerage firm. As time goes on, you'll discover that your total contribution figure has little meaning in relation to portfolio value. If you learn your investment lessons well, your portfolio value should far exceed the amount of your contributions.

### Determining Unit Value

Each month, your financial report should show the opening market value of your club's portfolio—the current price of the stocks your club owns, plus any cash in your money market account. Your treasurer will take this information from your brokerage firm's monthly report. As an example, assume that this month's market value of your club's portfolio is $2,100, and that your club has a total of 80.000 beginning units of ownership (8 members × 10.000 units each). Divide your club's current portfolio value of $2,100 by your club's total units (80.000), which gives you a new unit value of $26.25. Since the market value of your club's portfolio and the number of units of ownership will change monthly, your treasurer must calculate your club's unit value every month. Like the stock market, it is constantly changing.

8 Members × 10 Units = 80 Beginning units of ownership

$2,100 Portfolio value ÷ 80.000 Units
= $26.25 Current value of 1 unit

*Note:* If members have differing units of ownership, you cannot multiply the number of members by the number of units they own. You must *add* each member's units to determine the total number of units owned in your club.

### Determining Number of Units Monthly Contribution Will Buy

After calculating your club's new unit value for the month to be $26.25, the treasurer must determine the amount of units your current month's $25 investment contribution will purchase. To do this, divide your $25 contribution by the current month's unit value of $26.25. Thus,

0.952 of one unit of ownership would be added to last month's 10.000 units, giving you a new total of 10.952 units of ownership in your club.

$25.00 Monthly contribution
÷ $26.25 Unit value for current month
= 0.952 Units your $25 contribution will buy

Then add this month's units to your total units, or base units, as shown in Figure 7.1.

10.000 Original units
+ 0.952 New units for the month
= 10.952 Total units of ownership in the club this month

## *Calculating Membership or Individual Net Value in Club*

To determine net value in your club, simply multiply the total number of units you own by the current month's market value of one unit.

10.952 Units × $26.25 = $287.49

So look at the individual net column in Figure 7.1; each member's individual contribution of $275 is worth $287.49 this month!

10.952 Units owned
× $ 26.25 Current value of one unit
= $287.49 Individual net value

## *Making Timely Investment Contributions*

Figure 7.3 illustrates the importance of making your investment contributions on time. Susan missed February's meeting and waited until March to pay her February contribution. So in March she has made the same total contributions as her fellow members. However, February's unit value was $26.25, which meant her $25 contribution would have purchased more units than in March when the value of one unit was $28.25. Thus, Susan's ownership in the club is

**FIGURE 7.3**    Example of Timely Investment Contributions

**Financial Report: January 15, 1994**

Membership Value
Portfolio Value: $2,000.00

Beginning portfolio value/total base units = $ value per unit
($2,000 ÷ 80.000 = $25.00)

| Name | Total Contribution | Base Units | New Units | Total Units | % Club Owned | Market Value/Unit | Individual Net |
|------|-------------------|-----------|-----------|-------------|--------------|-------------------|----------------|
| Susan | $ 250.00 | 10.000 | | 10.000 | 12.50 | $25.00 | $ 250.00 |
| Alice | $ 250.00 | 10.000 | | 10.000 | 12.50 | $25.00 | $ 250.00 |
| Mary | $ 250.00 | 10.000 | | 10.000 | 12.50 | $25.00 | $ 250.00 |
| Ann | $ 250.00 | 10.000 | | 10.000 | 12.50 | $25.00 | $ 250.00 |
| Nancy | $ 250.00 | 10.000 | | 10.000 | 12.50 | $25.00 | $ 250.00 |
| Diane | $ 250.00 | 10.000 | | 10.000 | 12.50 | $25.00 | $ 250.00 |
| Jean | $ 250.00 | 10.000 | | 10.000 | 12.50 | $25.00 | $ 250.00 |
| Carol | $ 250.00 | 10.000 | | 10.000 | 12.50 | $25.00 | $ 250.00 |
| **Total** | **$2,000.00** | **80.000** | | **80.000** | **100.00** | | **$2,000.00** |

**FIGURE 7.3** (Continued)

**Financial Report: February 15, 1994**

Membership Value
Portfolio Value: $2,100.00

Portfolio value/total base units = $ value per unit

($2,100 ÷ 80.000 = $26.25)

New individual contribution/$ value per unit = new units

($25 ÷ $26.25 = 0.952)

| Name | Total Contribution | Base Units | New Units | Total Units | % Club Owned | Market Value/Unit | Individual Net |
|---|---|---|---|---|---|---|---|
| **Susan** | **$ 250.00** | **10.000** | **0** | **10.000** | **11.54** | **$26.25** | **$ 262.50** |
| Alice | $ 275.00 | 10.000 | 0.952 | 10.952 | 12.64 | $26.25 | $ 287.49 |
| Mary | $ 275.00 | 10.000 | 0.952 | 10.952 | 12.64 | $26.25 | $ 287.49 |
| Ann | $ 275.00 | 10.000 | 0.952 | 10.952 | 12.64 | $26.25 | $ 287.49 |
| Nancy | $ 275.00 | 10.000 | 0.952 | 10.952 | 12.64 | $26.25 | $ 287.49 |
| Diane | $ 275.00 | 10.000 | 0.952 | 10.952 | 12.64 | $26.25 | $ 287.49 |
| Jean | $ 275.00 | 10.000 | 0.952 | 10.952 | 12.64 | $26.25 | $ 287.49 |
| Carol | $ 275.00 | 10.000 | 0.952 | 10.952 | 12.64 | $26.25 | $ 287.49 |
| **Total** | **$2,175.00** | **80.000** | **6.664** | **86.664** | **100.00** | | **$2,274.93** |

FIGURE 7.3  Example of Timely Investment Contributions (Continued)

## Financial Report: March 15, 1994

Membership Value
Portfolio Value: $2,500.00

Portfolio value/total base units = $ value per unit

($2,500 ÷ 86.664 = $28.85)

New individual contribution/$ value per unit = new units

($25 ÷ $28.85 = 0.867)

| Name | Total Contribution | Base Units | New Units | Total Units | % Club Owned | Market Value/Unit | Individual Net |
|---|---|---|---|---|---|---|---|
| **Susan** | **$ 300.00** | **10.000** | ***1.733** | **11.733** | **12.42** | **$28.85** | **$ 338.50** |
| Alice | $ 300.00 | 10.952 | 0.867 | 11.819 | 12.51 | $28.85 | $ 340.98 |
| Mary | $ 300.00 | 10.952 | 0.867 | 11.819 | 12.51 | $28.85 | $ 340.98 |
| Ann | $ 300.00 | 10.952 | 0.867 | 11.819 | 12.51 | $28.85 | $ 340.98 |
| Nancy | $ 300.00 | 10.952 | 0.867 | 11.819 | 12.51 | $28.85 | $ 340.98 |
| Diane | $ 300.00 | 10.952 | 0.867 | 11.819 | 12.51 | $28.85 | $ 340.98 |
| Jean | $ 300.00 | 10.952 | 0.867 | 11.819 | 12.51 | $28.85 | $ 340.98 |
| Carol | $ 300.00 | 10.952 | 0.867 | 11.819 | 12.51 | $28.85 | $ 340.98 |
| **Total** | **$2,400.00** | **86.664** | **7.802** | **94.466** | **100.00** | | **$2,725.36** |

*$50 Contribution/$28.85 = 1.733 units

less. To ensure that all members have equal value, contributions must be made on time. If you plan to miss a meeting, give your contribution to your treasurer in time to ensure that it is deposited with other members' investment contributions.

Make sure that you understand how your portfolio's value affects unit value and the resultant individual member's net value. Now that you can see how important it is to make timely contributions, the beauty of the unit accounting system is that its formula easily allows for late contributions and the addition of new members.

# Tips for Success

Provide Members with the Report Before Your Meetings

Study the Report until You Understand It

Have Current Stock Prices Available

# DESIGNING A FINANCIAL REPORT THAT REFLECTS YOUR BOTTOM LINE:
## Long and Short Forms

$\mathcal{N}$ow that you understand unit and membership value, you are ready to create financial reports. These reports are vital—they are a photograph of your club's successes and failures: How much money you've contributed, how you have invested these contributions and how your investments have performed. They should be filed in a binder for safekeeping and given to a new treasurer, whenever one is elected, for these reports are an important part of your club's history. Each month your treasurer must gather your club's pertinent financial information from the brokerage firm's monthly statement and translate that data into an accurate, comprehensible report. Having a computer spreadsheet program available will certainly make preparing these reports both easier and faster. Another helpful resource is the NAIC's *Club Accounting Kit,* which provides complete instructions to keep investment club records.

## The Full Report

Your treasurer should prepare and distribute this full report to all club members until they have a good understanding of the unit accounting system, which we looked at in Chapter 7. A sample of the full financial report appears in Figure 8.1. Let's examine each of the four parts of the report.

### *Part I*

The first part of the report (see Figure 8.2) is a simple accounting of each member's contributions, beginning with an ending balance from the prior year and continuing with the current year's contributions listed by month. The last column in the section reflects the total amount each member has contributed since joining your club. For example, Susan had contributed $250 by the end of 1994 and $25 in January 1995 for a total of $275 contributed so far to the club.

### *Part II*

The second section of the financial report, entitled "Portfolio" (see Figure 8.3), accounts for each stock in your club's portfolio: (The date and number of shares purchased, price per share, commission fees, dividends reinvested, any additional shares you've purchased, plus any stock splits that have occurred, plus any additional shares you've purchased.) The last three columns in this section state the total number of shares of each stock you own, the total amount you have invested and the average cost per share. As you can see, the price per share multiplied by the number of shares purchased (e.g., XYZ Co.: 25 shares × $30 per share = $750) differs from the total amount invested. That's because commission fees are included in the "amount invested to date" column ($750 + $35 commission = $785). To determine the average cost per share, shown in the last column, divide the dollar amount found in the "amount invested to date" column (which includes commissions) by the number of shares purchased ($785 ÷ 25 shares = $31.40). Thus, your average cost per share will be higher than the actual per share price multiplied by the number of shares purchased. It's a good idea to abbreviate the stock's name as it appears in the newspaper or add the stock's ticker symbol, so that members become familiar with the way the stock is quoted and can find it easily.

The lower portion of Part II accounts for your stock sales. This section tracks when your club decides to remove a stock from your club's portfolio. The important column in this section is the "(less commission)" figure, which is what you pay the broker for selling the stock. You then subtract this figure from the total dollar amount of the sale. In this illustration your cost basis for FLYHI stock was $393. This is the total amount you spent to purchase the stock:

| | |
|---|---|
| 25 shares × $14.38 per share | $359.50 |
| Plus: commission charge | 33.50 |
| Total cost | $393.00 |

The bottom portion of Figure 8.3 outlines the sale of your FLYHI stock:

| | |
|---|---|
| Sell 25 shares at $12.75 per share | $318.75 |
| Subtract: commission | 33.00 |
| Total received | $285.75 |

As you can see in Figure 8.3, the total shares sold (25) multiplied by $12.75 (price per share at the time of sale) equals $318.75. When you subtract the commission charge of $33 from $318.75, you have a balance of $285.75. Unfortunately, in this illustration you paid $393 (including the commission for buying the stock) for the stock FLYHI, so you've lost $107.25 or –27 percent.

**FIGURE 8.1**    Sample of Full Financial Report

Financial Report
Your Investment Club
(Date)

**PART I: Contributions**

Contributions—1995

| Name | 1994 Balance | Jan | Feb | Mar | Apr | May | Jun | Jul | Aug | Sep | Oct | Nov | Dec | Total |
|------|---------|-----|-----|-----|-----|-----|-----|-----|-----|-----|-----|-----|-----|-------|
| Susan | $ 250.00 | $ 25.00 | | | | | | | | | | | | $ 275.00 |
| Alice | $ 250.00 | $ 25.00 | | | | | | | | | | | | $ 275.00 |
| Mary | $ 250.00 | $ 25.00 | | | | | | | | | | | | $ 275.00 |
| Ann | $ 250.00 | $ 25.00 | | | | | | | | | | | | $ 275.00 |
| Nancy | $ 250.00 | $ 25.00 | | | | | | | | | | | | $ 275.00 |
| Diane | $ 250.00 | $ 25.00 | | | | | | | | | | | | $ 275.00 |
| Jean | $ 250.00 | $ 25.00 | | | | | | | | | | | | $ 275.00 |
| Carol | $ 250.00 | $ 25.00 | | | | | | | | | | | | $ 275.00 |
| **Total** | **$2,000.00** | **$200.00** | | | | | | | | | | | | **$2,200.00** |

## Part II: Portfolio

### Purchases

| Stock | Date of Purchase | Number Shares | Price/ Share | Comm. | Reinvest Div/Cap Gains | Add Invest | Add Sh Bt Split | Total Shares | Amount Invested To Date | Average Cost/Share |
|---|---|---|---|---|---|---|---|---|---|---|
| XYZ CO | 5/23/92 | 25 | $30.00 | $35.00 | | | | 25 | $785.00 | $31.40 |
| SSAIL | 8/20/92 | 25 | $24.25 | $35.00 | | | | 25 | $641.25 | $25.65 |
| BB CO | 2/15/93 | 100 | $ 2.13 | $31.88 | | | | 100 | $244.88 | $ 2.45 |

### Sales

| Stock | Date Sold | Number Shares | Price/ Share | (Less Commission) | Total Received | Cost | Net | % Gain/Loss |
|---|---|---|---|---|---|---|---|---|
| FLYHI | 9/15/92 | 25 | $12.75 | ($33.00) | $285.75 | $393.00 | ($107.25) | (27) |

**FIGURE 8.1**   Sample of Full Financial Report (Continued)

Date prepared: _____ Using _____ Brokerage Statement
(Date)

**PART III: Current Activity**

| Stock | Number Shares | Purchase Price Share | Current Share Price | Cash Dividend Year-to-Date | Total Current Value | Total Cost | % Gain/ Loss | % Gain/ Loss | Stop Loss |
|---|---|---|---|---|---|---|---|---|---|
| XYZ CO. | 25 | $30.00 | $40.00 | | $1,000.00 | $ 785.00 | 215.00 | 27.39 | $34.50 |
| SSAIL | 25 | $24.25 | $21.25 | | $ 531.25 | $ 641.25 | (110.00) | (17.15) | $19.75 |
| BB CO | 100 | $ 2.13 | $ 3.00 | | $ 300.00 | $ 244.88 | 55.12 | 22.51 | $ 2.50 |
| **Total** | | | | | **$1,831.25** | **$1,671.13** | **160.12** | **9.58** | |

Beginning cash: $ 268.75
Value of investments: $1,831.25
Current portfolio value: $2,100.00
Plus new contributions: $ 200.00
Total value of club: $2,300.00

## PART IV: Membership Value

Portfolio Value: $2,100.00

Portfolio value/total base units = $ value per unit

($2,100 ÷ 80,000 = $26.25 per unit)

New individual contribution/$ value per unit = new units

($25 contribution ÷ $26.25 = 0.925 unit)

| Name | Total Contributions | Base Units | New Units | Total Units | % Club Owned | Market Value/ Units | Individual Net | Individual Gain/Loss | % Individual Gain/Loss |
|------|--------------------|-----------|-----------|-------------|--------------|---------------------|----------------|---------------------|------------------------|
| Susan | $ 275.00 | 10.000 | 0.952 | 10.952 | 12.50 | $26.25 | $ 287.49 | $12.49 | 4.54 |
| Alice | $ 275.00 | 10.000 | 0.952 | 10.952 | 12.50 | $26.25 | $ 287.49 | $12.49 | 4.54 |
| Mary | $ 275.00 | 10.000 | 0.952 | 10.952 | 12.50 | $26.25 | $ 287.49 | $12.49 | 4.54 |
| Ann | $ 275.00 | 10.000 | 0.952 | 10.952 | 12.50 | $26.25 | $ 287.49 | $12.49 | 4.54 |
| Nancy | $ 275.00 | 10.000 | 0.952 | 10.952 | 12.50 | $26.25 | $ 287.49 | $12.49 | 4.54 |
| Diane | $ 275.00 | 10.000 | 0.952 | 10.952 | 12.50 | $26.25 | $ 287.49 | $12.49 | 4.54 |
| Jean | $ 275.00 | 10.000 | 0.952 | 10.952 | 12.50 | $26.25 | $ 287.49 | $12.49 | 4.54 |
| Carol | $ 275.00 | 10.000 | 0.952 | 10.952 | 12.50 | $26.25 | $ 287.49 | $12.49 | 4.54 |
| **Total** | **$2,200.00** | **80.000** | **7.616** | **87.616** | **100.00** | | **$2,299.92** | **$99.92** | |

**FIGURE 8.2**  Sample of Financial Report "Contributions" Section

**Financial Report**
**Your Investment Club**
(Date)

**PART I: Contributions**

Contributions—1995

| Name | 1994 Balance | Jan | Feb | Mar | Apr | May | Jun | Jul | Aug | Sep | Oct | Nov | Dec | Total |
|---|---|---|---|---|---|---|---|---|---|---|---|---|---|---|
| Susan | $ 250.00 | $ 25.00 | | | | | | | | | | | | $ 275.00 |
| Alice | $ 250.00 | $ 25.00 | | | | | | | | | | | | $ 275.00 |
| Mary | $ 250.00 | $ 25.00 | | | | | | | | | | | | $ 275.00 |
| Ann | $ 250.00 | $ 25.00 | | | | | | | | | | | | $ 275.00 |
| Nancy | $ 250.00 | $ 25.00 | | | | | | | | | | | | $ 275.00 |
| Diane | $ 250.00 | $ 25.00 | | | | | | | | | | | | $ 275.00 |
| Jean | $ 250.00 | $ 25.00 | | | | | | | | | | | | $ 275.00 |
| Carol | $ 250.00 | $ 25.00 | | | | | | | | | | | | $ 275.00 |
| **Total** | **$2,000.00** | **$200.00** | | | | | | | | | | | | **$2,200.00** |

**FIGURE 8.3**  Sample of Financial Report "Portfolio" Section

**Part II: Portfolio**

**Purchases**

| Stock | Date of Purchase | Number Shares | Price/ Share | Comm. | Reinvest Div/Cap Gains | Add Invest | Add Sh Bt Split | Total Shares | Amt Inv. To Date | Average Cost/Share |
|---|---|---|---|---|---|---|---|---|---|---|
| XYZ CO | 5/23/92 | 25 | $30.00 | $35.00 | | | | 25 | $785.00 | $31.40 |
| SSAIL | 8/20/92 | 25 | $24.25 | $35.00 | | | | 25 | $641.25 | $25.65 |
| BB CO | 2/15/93 | 100 | $ 2.13 | $31.88 | | | | 100 | $244.88 | $ 2.45 |

**Sales**

| Stock | Date Sold | Number Shares | Price/ Share | (Less Commission) | Total Received | Cost | Net | % Gain/Loss |
|---|---|---|---|---|---|---|---|---|
| FLYHI | 9/15/92 | 25 | $12.75 | ($33.00) | $285.75 | $393.00 | ($107.25) | (27) |

## Part III

The third part of the financial report is entitled "current activity." This is a record of what has occurred in your portfolio during the past month except for the dividend column, which reflects dividends received year-to-date. This section includes the number of shares your club currently owns, the per-share price at the time you bought the stock, the current price per share, dividends received and this month's value of your stocks. The "total cost" column reflects the amount you paid for each stock, including commissions. The next two columns show your gains or losses for each stock as a dollar amount and as a percentage of your total cost. Below are two examples showing you how to calculate these figures using XYZ and SSAIL:

XYZ's Total current value   =   $1,000
Less: total cost            =        785
Profit                      =   $   215
($215 ÷ $785 = $0.27 profit on this investment)

SSAIL's Total current value   =   $531.25
Less: total cost              =      641.25
Profit                            ($110.00)
($110 ÷ $641.25 = $0.17 loss on this investment)

The last column is titled "stop loss." The stop loss figures, explained in more detail in Chapter 13, are the price points at which you decide in advance to sell the stock.

Below these columns is the amount of cash in your account that you have not yet invested and the total value of the stocks you currently own. Added together, these two figures equal the total current value of your club. Because your treasurer will obtain all the information in this section from your brokerage firm's monthly report to your club, your financial report probably will reflect stock prices that are a week or so old so your treasurer should bring updated prices to report at your meetings. When our treasurer presents her report, she merely reads our stocks' closing prices

**FIGURE 8.4**   Sample of Financial Report "Current Activity" Section

**PART III: Current Activity**

| Stock | Number Shares | Cost per Share | Current Share Price | Cash Dividend Year-to-Date | Total Current Value | Total Cost | % Gain/ Loss | % Gain/ Loss | Stop Loss |
|---|---|---|---|---|---|---|---|---|---|
| XYZ CO. | 25 | $30.00 | $40.00 | | $1,000.00 | $ 785.00 | 215.00 | 27.39 | $34.50 |
| SSAIL | 25 | $24.25 | $21.25 | | $ 531.25 | $ 641.25 | (110.00) | (17.15) | $19.75 |
| BB CO | 100 | $ 2.13 | $ 3.00 | | $ 300.00 | $ 244.88 | 55.12 | 22.51 | $ 2.50 |
| **Total** | | | | | **$1,831.25** | **$1,671.13** | **160.12** | **9.58** | |

Beginning cash: $ 268.75
Value of investments: $1,831.25
Current portfolio value: $2,100.00
Plus new contributions: $ 200.00
Total value of club: $2,300.00

for the day or the preceding day, and we write them in the margin of this section of the financial report. The last two lines of this section show $200 in contributions that have not yet been deposited in your brokerage account, which when added to the club's current portfolio value gives you a total value for the club.

### Part IV

Finally, the last section of the financial report is a determination of each member's value in the club. Chapter 7 explains how you calculate this information using the unit accounting system.

### Determining Performance

Many people find thinking in terms of percentages more meaningful than actual dollars. Would you be interested in analyzing a stock whose earnings per share are predicted to increase to $0.52 next year? Or would you be more inclined to look at that stock if you knew its earnings were predicted to increase 14 percent?

The bottom portion of Part II in Figure 8.1 shows a 27 percent loss on the sale of the FLYHI stock. Part III has a column that reflects the percent gain or loss of a stock's total current value since the date of purchase. And Part IV indicates each member's percent gain or loss of value in the club itself. You'll also want to calculate the percentage of growth or decline of sales and earnings of a company whose stock you are considering for purchase.

**Calculating Net Loss**    The discussion of Part III of the financial report showed you how to calculate a loss using SSAIL as an example. The way to determine a loss is to subtract the amount you receive on the sale of a stock from the amount you paid. You then divide this difference by your original or beginning cost figure. To illustrate, the bottom portion of Part II shows the 25 shares of FLYHI stock that were purchased for $393 (including commission). When

**FIGURE 8.5**   Financial Report "Membership Value" Section

## PART IV: Membership Value

Portfolio Value: $2,100.00

Portfolio value/total base units = $ value per unit

($2,100 ÷ 80,000 = $26.25 per unit)

New individual contribution/$ value per unit = new units

($25 contribution ÷ $26.25 = 0.925 unit)

| Name | Total Contributions | Base Units | New Units | Total Units | % Club Owned | Market Value/ Units | Individual Net | Individual Gain/Loss | % Individual Gain/Loss |
|---|---|---|---|---|---|---|---|---|---|
| Susan | $ 275.00 | 10.000 | 0.952 | 10.952 | 12.50 | $26.25 | $ 287.49 | $12.49 | 4.54 |
| Alice | $ 275.00 | 10.000 | 0.952 | 10.952 | 12.50 | $26.25 | $ 287.49 | $12.49 | 4.54 |
| Mary | $ 275.00 | 10.000 | 0.952 | 10.952 | 12.50 | $26.25 | $ 287.49 | $12.49 | 4.54 |
| Ann | $ 275.00 | 10.000 | 0.952 | 10.952 | 12.50 | $26.25 | $ 287.49 | $12.49 | 4.54 |
| Nancy | $ 275.00 | 10.000 | 0.952 | 10.952 | 12.50 | $26.25 | $ 287.49 | $12.49 | 4.54 |
| Diane | $ 275.00 | 10.000 | 0.952 | 10.952 | 12.50 | $26.25 | $ 287.49 | $12.49 | 4.54 |
| Jean | $ 275.00 | 10.000 | 0.952 | 10.952 | 12.50 | $26.25 | $ 287.49 | $12.49 | 4.54 |
| Carol | $ 275.00 | 10.000 | 0.952 | 10.952 | 12.50 | $26.25 | $ 287.49 | $12.49 | 4.54 |
| **Total** | **$2,200.00** | **80.000** | **7.616** | **87.616** | **100.00** | | **$2,299.92** | **$99.92** | |

your club sold these same shares, it received a total of $285.75 (after deducting commissions). This resulted in a dollar loss of $107.25.

To determine this dollar loss as a percent, divide the loss of $107.25 by the original total cost of $393: Thus, you experienced a 27 percent loss on your investment.

$285.75 Sales price – $393 Cost price = ($107.25) Loss

($107.27) Dollar loss ÷ $393 Original price = 27% Loss

**Calculating Increased Stock Value**    In Part III of the financial report, you can see that the club purchased XYZ's stock for a total cost of $785. This month, the stock's shares are valued at $1,000; a 27.39% increase in your investment. To determine this percentage, subtract the cost value from this month's value which results in a $215 increase in the value of the stock.

$1,000 Current value – $785 Total cost
= $215 Increase in value

$215 Increased value ÷ $785 Original cost
= 27.39% Increase in stock's value

You then divide this $215 increase by your original "total cost" to determine net gain.

We show these percentages on our financial reports as an indication of how well or poorly our investments are doing. Since we are not actually selling the stocks, we do not include a commission charge for selling the stock when calculating these percentages. However, we do factor sales commissions into the calculation when we actually make the trade

**Determining membership Value**    Each member's value in your club has increased by 4.54 percent, according to Part IV of the financial report. This percentage is determined by subtracting the member's total contributions from his or her current net value. You then divide the member's increased value by the amount of his or her total contributions:

$287.49 Individual net value – $275 Individual total
contribution = $12.49 Increased net value

$12.49 Increased net value ÷ $275 Total contribution
= 4.54% Gain in membership value

## Calculating Earnings Per Share

Earnings per share (EPS) are a very important figure to examine when analyzing a stock. This figure represents a company's profitability, and it is calculated by dividing a company's net earnings into the number of shares out-standing.

To determine a company's estimated increase or de-crease in EPS as a percentage, let's assume that ABC's 1994 earnings were $3.78 per share, and they are estimated to be $4.30 in 1995. We would subtract 1994's EPS from 1995's estimated EPS and divide our answer by 1994's EPS:

> ABC Company
> Estimated 1995 EPS  = $4.30
> Less: 1994 EPS      =  3.78
> Total projected gain = $0.52

($0.52 divided by $3.78 = 13.7% estimated increase in EPS)

To determine these percentages, you must always sub-tract your beginning number from your current number and divide your answer by the beginning, or base, number as shown in the following examples.

Now it's your turn. Let's take Coca-Cola as an example. Coke's 1994 earnings per share were $2.00, and they are projected to be $2.30 in 1995. Can you determine the esti-mated percentage of earnings growth? If you said 15 percent, you're right!

Our treasurer calculates the percent increase or de-crease in the value of each stock in our portfolio and each member's percent increase in net value every month, so that these figures can be included in our financial reports. It's not a daunting task if your treasurer has a spreadsheet program; all he or she has to do is enter the numbers into the spreadsheet program and let the computer do the rest.

**FIGURE 8.6**   Determining Projected EPS Growth

**Measuring Performance**

|                              | 1994   | 1995 (estimated) |
|------------------------------|--------|------------------|
| 1. ABC Company               |        |                  |
| Earnings per share:          | $3.78  | $4.30            |

$$\begin{array}{r} \$4.30 \\ -3.78 \\ \hline \$0.52 \end{array}$$

$\dfrac{\$0.52}{\$3.78}$ = 13.7% increase in estimated earnings per share

|                              | 1994   | 1995 (estimated) |
|------------------------------|--------|------------------|
| 2. CCC, Inc.                 | $3.78  | $3.25            |
| Earnings per share:          |        |                  |

$$\begin{array}{r} \$\,3.25 \\ -\,3.78 \\ \hline \$(0.53) \end{array}$$

$\dfrac{\$(0.52)}{\$3.78}$ = 14% decrease in estimated earnings per share

Because it will take time for your membership to fully understand the financial report, try to include a copy with your mailing of the previous month's minutes, which are sent a week before your forthcoming meeting. By doing this, you'll give your members time to study the report on their own and, hopefully, eliminate what could be a stumbling block to well organized meetings.

## An Abbreviated Financial Report

Now that my club's members have a good understanding of the financial report and the unit accounting system, our treasurer has developed an abbreviated financial report, a sample of which is shown in Figure 8.7, which she distributes to all club members and reviews at our meetings. She continues to prepare a full report for the club's records; it is available to any member wishing to review it.

This condensed report consists of three sections. The first section combines parts I and IV of the full report and reflects membership value. The middle section contains information on the stocks currently in the club's portfolio, and the last section is an accounting of the cash activity for the month, plus the amount of money we have available to invest. Three figures in this abbreviated report are important:

1. *Total "individual net dollars," found in Part I of this report.* This is the total of each member's net value in the club, and it includes investment contributions (cash) not yet invested.
2. *"Total current value" found in Part II.* This figure is the current value of the stocks in the portfolio, less cash not invested.
3. *"Cash balance," which is found in Part III.* This figure represents the current amount of cash the club has available to purchase stocks.

This abbreviated financial report will allow you to quickly review your club's financial information so that you can spend more time discussing the individual stocks you currently own and those you are considering for purchase.

These financial reports are a valuable tool to determine how well your investments are performing. If your stocks are increasing in price, you will profit from the investment lessons you've learned as well as your membership in the investment club. At first, the reports will be difficult to understand; don't get lost in the numbers—they will become easier after you've worked with them a few times.

FIGURE 8.7   Sample of Abbreviated Financial Report

**Financial Report**
**Your Investment Club**

**Membership Value**

Date prepared: _____   Using (Brokerage Firm's) Statement Dated: _____

| Name | 1992 Balance | 1992 Deposits | Total Invested | Units Owned | % Owned | Individual Net $ | % + or − |
|------|-------------|---------------|----------------|-------------|---------|------------------|----------|
| Susan | $ 250.00 | 25.00 | 275.00 | 10.952 | 12.50 | $ 287.49 | 4.54 |
| Alice | $ 250.00 | 25.00 | 275.00 | 10.952 | 12.50 | $ 287.49 | 4.54 |
| Mary | $ 250.00 | 25.00 | 275.00 | 10.952 | 12.50 | $ 287.49 | 4.54 |
| Ann | $ 250.00 | 25.00 | 275.00 | 10.952 | 12.50 | $ 287.49 | 4.54 |
| Nancy | $ 250.00 | 25.00 | 275.00 | 10.952 | 12.50 | $ 287.49 | 4.54 |
| Diane | $ 250.00 | 25.00 | 275.00 | 10.952 | 12.50 | $ 287.49 | 4.54 |
| Jean | $ 250.00 | 25.00 | 275.00 | 10.952 | 12.50 | $ 287.49 | 4.54 |
| Carol | $ 250.00 | 25.00 | 275.00 | 10.952 | 12.50 | $ 287.49 | 4.54 |
| **Total** | **$2,000.00** | **$200.00** | **$2,200.00** | **87.616** | **100.00** | **$2,299.92** | |

## Current Portfolio

| Stock | Number Shares | Purchase Price Share | Current Share Price | Cash Dividend Year-to-Date | Total Current Value | Total Cost | % Gain/ Loss | % Gain/ Loss | Stop Loss |
|---|---|---|---|---|---|---|---|---|---|
| XYZ CO. | 25 | $30.00 | $40.00 | | $1,000.00 | $ 785.00 | 215.00 | 27.39 | $34.50 |
| SSAIL | 25 | $24.25 | $21.25 | | $ 531.25 | $ 641.25 | (110.00) | (17.15) | $19.75 |
| BB CO | 100 | $ 2.13 | $ 3.00 | | $ 300.00 | $ 244.88 | 55.12 | 22.51 | $ 2.50 |
| **Total** | | | | | **$1,831.25** | **$1,671.13** | **160.12** | **9.58** | |

### Cash Activity for Month:

| | |
|---|---|
| Beginning Cash Balance: | $268.75 |
| Income | |
| Member Contributions: | $200.00 |
| Dividends: | |
| Interest (Money market): | |
| Stock sales: | |
| Other: | |
| Total income: | $468.75 |
| Expenses | |
| Stock purchases: | |
| Other: | |
| Total expenses: | |
| Cash balance (date) | $468.75 |

# Tips for Success

Seek Members with Complementary Skills

Members Should Agree with Your Investment Philosophy

Provide New Members with Club Information Sheet

Help New Members Learn

# CHAPTER 9

# ADDING NEW MEMBERS AT A PRICE THEY CAN AFFORD

$\mathcal{A}$s stated earlier, most established investment clubs have 15 to 20 members, although the recommended number of founding members is closer to seven or eight. Starting your club with seven or eight friends or co-workers is a comfortable number and allows you time to build confidence in managing your club.

## Growing Your Club

A time will come when your club will benefit from having an increased membership. Certainly, the larger your membership, the more dollars you'll have available to invest in the stock market and the more members to share stock research responsibilities. Of course, having a larger membership also means that you'll have more people who can serve as officers. And new members may bring investment knowledge to share with your membership. Before you solicit new members, though, be certain that you're comfortable with your club's operation and its method of selecting, analyzing and making stock purchase decisions.

When you feel the time is right to expand your club's membership, compile a list of potential members and invite them to attend a meeting. You can draw your list of potential members from your prospective member list (see Figure 2.2). Make it clear to your guests that you are not seeking a commitment at this time, but merely are giving them an opportunity to see how your club operates. As an aside, these prospective members need not be your close friends. The tie that binds is your quest for investment knowledge, and you'll discover the added benefit of making new friends among your club members.

## Club Information Packet

Develop an information packet to outline the important aspects of your club for prospective members:

- Your club's articles of association or partnership agreement
- Mission statement
- Investment philosophy
- Names of current members
- Club's officers
- How often you meet
- Location and what time you meet
- Amount of monthly investment contributions
- Strategy for choosing stocks to study
- Copy of the club's most recent financial report

After the prospective members have had an opportunity to observe your club in action and review the information provided, they can inform you whether they wish to join.

## The Mechanics of Joining

The financial procedure for adding new members to your club is simple once you have a good understanding of the unit accounting system described in Chapter 7. You cannot expect new members to pay into your club the same amount your founding members have contributed thus far. Indeed, contributions totaling $2,000 may be worth $2,100 or $1,800 today, depending upon the current market value of your investments.

As illustrated in Figure 9.1, if you added Joan as a new member last month, she would have made the same $25 monthly investment contribution as you made. Because last month was her first month as a member, however, she was starting with 0 base units, while the other members had a total of 10 base units. According to last month's unit value calculation, each member's $25 investment contribution purchased 0.952 units in the club. Therefore, because Joan was starting with 0 units, this month's financial report will show that she only owns 0.952 units in the club (0 beginning units + 0.952 units), while the other members own 10.952 units (10 base units + 0.952 units).

Don't forget: Each new member should make the same contribution as you have made that year to your club's checking account to help defray administrative expenses.

Understanding the mechanics of joining a club is important, but just as vital is making new members feel comfortable. Many may feel inadequate because they have little or no investment knowledge. Older members must take responsibility for teaching new members the lessons they've already learned. Share investment articles or spend an hour at lunch discussing investment topics with new members. The important thing is to be supportive and stress that you've all been new members at one time.

FIGURE 9.1   Unit Value Calculation for a New Member

## Financial Report: (Date)

Membership Value
Portfolio Value: $2,100.00
Portfolio value ÷ total base units = $ value per unit
($2,100 ÷ 80.000 = $26.25)
New individual contribution ÷ $ value per unit = new units
($25 ÷ $26.25 = 0.952)

| Name | Total Contribution | Base Units | New Units | Total Units | % Club Owned | Market Value | Individual Net |
|---|---|---|---|---|---|---|---|
| Susan | $ 275.00 | 10.000 | 0.952 | 10.952 | 12.37 | $26.25 | $ 287.49 |
| Alice | $ 275.00 | 10.000 | 0.952 | 10.952 | 12.37 | $26.25 | $ 287.49 |
| Mary | $ 275.00 | 10.000 | 0.952 | 10.952 | 12.37 | $26.25 | $ 287.49 |
| Ann | $ 275.00 | 10.000 | 0.952 | 10.952 | 12.37 | $26.25 | $ 287.49 |
| Nancy | $ 275.00 | 10.000 | 0.952 | 10.952 | 12.37 | $26.25 | $ 287.49 |
| Diane | $ 275.00 | 10.000 | 0.952 | 10.952 | 12.37 | $26.25 | $ 287.49 |
| Jean | $ 275.00 | 10.000 | 0.952 | 10.952 | 12.37 | $26.25 | $ 287.49 |
| Carol | $ 275.00 | 10.000 | 0.952 | 10.952 | 12.37 | $26.25 | $ 287.49 |
| Joan | $ 25.00 | 0.000 | 0.952 | 0.952 | 1.07 | $26.25 | $ 24.99 |
| Total | $2,225.00 | 80.000 | 8.568 | 88.568 | 100.00 | | $2,324.91 |

## Making Your Membership a Dynamic Group

Membership dynamics are important to keep in mind so that your club members work well together and the club profits. As you expand your membership, you'll be faced with as many different personalities as you have members. Your president must develop strong "people skills" to effectively handle Nancy Know-It-All, Deborah DoLittle and Susan Social. If your club does not run smoothly or you don't foresee or solve problems as they arise, members will become disenchanted and resign.

Just how do you deal with a Deborah DoLittle? There's no one way or right way. However, when a member of my club wasn't willing to do her fair share, it put a burden on the rest of us. Our president, sensing a problem, made a point of devoting extra time at one of our meetings for a general discussion on membership commitment and responsibility. Without pointing a finger, the member to whom the discussion was directed got the point and resigned. Since our membership is limited to 20, her resignation allowed us to take in a new member who was eager to make a commitment to our club.

Investment club membership is seldom static. Because our society is so mobile, it's important that your club can act quickly to fill a vacancy. Having a list of prospective members at your fingertips and packets of club information available will enable you to add members who have an important contribution to make to your club.

# Tips for Success

Don't Take a Resignation Personally

Don't Delay Reading a Resignation Letter

Wait Until You Have Cash To Pay a Resigning Member

CHAPTER 10

# PAYING RESIGNING MEMBERS THEIR FAIR SHARE

*I*t's imperative that your club maintain its membership so that you have adequate monthly contributions with which to buy stocks and enough members to share the work load. The best way to sustain a strong membership is by generating interest and enthusiasm. Inevitably, though, members will resign. Using Carol as an example, Figure 10.1 shows you how to determine a resigning member's share of ownership in the club.

Before any member can resign, he or she must first submit a letter of resignation to one of your officers. The officer who receives the letter will read it at your next regularly scheduled meeting. Then, in accordance with your club's partnership agreement or articles of association, your financial report for the meeting following the announcement of the member's resignation will reflect that member's net value in your club (the current market value of one unit multiplied by the number of units the resigning member owns). This is the amount due the resigning member.

Paragraph 9 of the sample articles of association and paragraph 13 of the partnership agreement (found in appendixes A and B, respectively) state that your club has ninety (90) days from the date of the *evaluation* (the financial report that is presented at the next regularly scheduled meeting after the resignation is announced) in which to pay the amount due the resigning member. The additional 90 days' time to make payment enables your club to accumulate cash in the form of monthly investment contributions rather than having to sell securities to pay a departing member his or her fair share.

FIGURE 10.1    Determining a Resigning Member's Ownership Share

## Financial Report: (Date)

Membership Value
Portfolio Value: $2,100.00
Portfolio value ÷ total base units = $ value per unit
($2,100 ÷ 80.000 = $26.25)
New individual contribution ÷ $ value per unit = new units
($25.00 ÷ $26.25 = 0.952)

| Name | Total Contribution | Base Units | New Units | Total Units | % Club Owned | Market Value | Individual Net |
|------|-------------------|-----------|-----------|-------------|--------------|--------------|----------------|
| Susan | $ 275.00 | 10.000 | 0.952 | 10.952 | 12.37 | $26.25 | $ 287.49 |
| Alice | $ 275.00 | 10.000 | 0.952 | 10.952 | 12.37 | $26.25 | $ 287.49 |
| Mary | $ 275.00 | 10.000 | 0.952 | 10.952 | 12.37 | $26.25 | $ 287.49 |
| Ann | $ 275.00 | 10.000 | 0.952 | 10.952 | 12.37 | $26.25 | $ 287.49 |
| Nancy | $ 275.00 | 10.000 | 0.952 | 10.952 | 12.37 | $26.25 | $ 287.49 |
| Diane | $ 275.00 | 10.000 | 0.952 | 10.952 | 12.37 | $26.25 | $ 287.49 |
| Jean | $ 275.00 | 10.000 | 0.952 | 10.952 | 12.37 | $26.25 | $ 287.49 |
| Carol | $ 275.00 | 10.000 | 0.952 | 10.952 | 12.37 | $26.25 | $ 287.49 |
| Joan | $ 25.00 | 0.000 | 0.952 | 0.952 | 1.07 | $26.25 | $ 24.99 |
| Total | $2,225.00 | 80.000 | 8.568 | 88.568 | 100.00 | | $2,324.91 |

# Tips for Success

Continue To Educate

Plan Ahead

Respond to Members' Needs

CHAPTER **11**

# DISCOVERING THE SECRETS OF LONG-TERM SUCCESS

$\mathcal{T}$he key to maintaining your members' interest and enthusiasm is to provide a continuing education in the stock market. If members think they might miss an important investment lesson, they'll make every effort to attend your investment club meetings. However, providing this education involves planning.

## Set Up a Steering Committee

At the beginning of the year, form a committee of three or four members to map out plans for the year ahead. This committee should seek input from all of you:

- What are your special investment interests?
- What investment topics would you like to know more about?

- Do you know guest speakers who could address your club?
- Are you happy with the way the club is structured?
- Do you have suggestions as to how the club can perform better?
- Can you suggest better ways to share investment information?
- Are you pleased with the way the club selects stocks to analyze?
- What industries do you think will do well in the coming year?

After your steering committee gathers suggestions and brainstorms ideas, they should create an annual plan. A sample planning guide is shown in Figure 11.1. Yours need not be this structured, but having an overall plan for the year will help you stay on track.

Here are some suggested steering committee responsibilities:

- *Develop a record of members' special investment interests and educational needs.* You may find some members still struggling with the important figures you use to analyze a company whose stock you are considering for purchase. Remember, some members may be fairly new in your club and won't have the experience analyzing stocks that you have. Other members may be interested in learning about investments other than stocks, such as bonds or mutual funds.
- *Arrange for speakers such as stockbrokers (your club's or others), economists and bankers to address your club several times during the year.* Use your record of members' special investment interests and educational needs as topics for these speakers to present to your membership.
- *Draft a list of suggested industries to research during the year.* Financial newspapers, magazines and Value Line are sources to help you create this list (discussed in the following chapter).

**FIGURE 11.1**   Sample Yearly Planning Guide

## Planning Guide

| January | February | March |
|---|---|---|
| Ratify nominations: new officers | Industry presentation: drugstores | Industry presentation: manufactured |
| Distribute statement of gains/losses for personal income tax returns | Educational segment: how to read *The Wall Street Journal* | housing |
| Review past year's performance | | Stock purchase decisions |
| Industry presentation: medical services | | Portfolio review |
| **April** | **May** | **June** |
| Industry presentation: electronics | Guest speaker | Industry presentation: metals and mining |
| Educational segment: review of financial magazines | Industry presentation: chemicals | Stock purchase decisions |
| | | Portfolio review |
| | | Industries to study next six months |
| **July** | **August** | **September** |
| Industry presentation: computer software | Industry presentation: computer and peripherals | Industry presentation: semiconductors |
| Educational segment: annual reports | Educational segment: to be decided | Stock purchase decisions |
| | | Educational segment: to be decided |
| **October** | **November** | **December** |
| Guest speaker | Industry presentation: advertising | Appoint nominating committee |
| Industry presentation: beverage | Educational segment: to be decided | Stock purchase decisions |
| | | Industries to study next six months |
| | | Comments/suggestions |

- *At the end of each year, present a slate of officers to serve the coming year.* The proposed officers should agree to serve before you seek approval from your full membership. Officers shouldn't serve in the same capacity for more than two years in a row—they tend to lose their zeal. Besides, the load should be shared. You'll find new officers are eager to tackle their responsibilities and that energy is catching.

My club attempts to devote a certain amount of time at each meeting to investment education. In response to our members' educational needs, we've developed a list of special interest topics:

- Learning how to read *The Wall Street Journal*
- Reviewing selected financial magazines
- Learning how to read an annual report
- Learning how interest rates affect the stock market
- Explaining the various figures found on the Value Line and Standard & Poor's reports and their significance
- Explaining what bonds are and how they differ from stocks
- Learning more about real estate investment trusts: what they are, and how they work
- Buying on margin: puts and calls

We ask one or two members to research the subject to be presented and make a report at a subsequent meeting. Often, our members will ask questions about the topic that our researchers cannot answer. When this happens and if enough members express interest in the topic, we will ask a guest speaker, or expert, to address our membership on the particular subject. We also share relevant investment articles, either distributing copies at our meetings or including them with the mailing of our meetings' minutes. Your club members want and need to learn—that may be part of the goal set forth in the club's mission statement. And many of your members will use the investment lessons they learn in their club experience to manage their own portfolios. So, if members can gain at least one piece of investment knowledge from a meeting, they'll feel that they have spent their time well, and they will have justified their decision to join the club.

## The Year in Review

At the end of each year, take time to discuss your accomplishments and failures. Entertain suggestions on how your club can better function: Do you need to add more members? Are you pleased with the way you select stocks to study? How have your investments performed? Review the stocks in your club's portfolio and your original reasons for purchasing them. Are these reasons still valid? Do the stocks in your club's portfolio conform with members' risk tolerance levels? Are you too heavily weighted in one particular industry? Also, your treasurer should provide you with an accounting of your gains or losses for the year, which you must report on your personal income tax return. Remember to make a concerted effort to incorporate these recommendations and ideas into actions during the coming year. This will make members feel they are an important part of their club, which in turn will help ensure the club's continued success.

## What Next?

At last! You've addressed the month-to-month operations of your investment club. Now starts your real education—it's time to invest your club's assets. In part III, I have drawn upon my investment club experiences to suggest ways to begin your adventure in the stock market. Also in part III, I suggest some ways to begin building a portfolio that are appropriate for investment clubs.

# Part Three

# BEGINNING TO INVEST WISELY

*If* a man empties his purse into his head,
no man can take it away from him.
An investment in knowledge always pays
the best interest.

*Benjamin Franklin*

# Tips for Success

Ask Your Broker for Assistance

Don't Act on Hot Tips

Buy What You Know

Pay Attention to your Portfolio

# CHAPTER 12

# BUILDING A PORTFOLIO FROM THE GROUND UP

$\mathcal{L}$iterally thousands of stocks are eager to be purchased. So now that you're ready to venture into the market where do you begin?

## Request Your Broker's Assistance

Invite your broker to attend a meeting and to bring enough copies of research materials on a recommended industry and a specific stock within that industry to study. Brokerage firms have research departments that provide the type of information you are asking your broker to bring to your meeting. If your broker is anxious to help you learn how to invest in the stock market, you should not have to pay him or her to attend any of your meetings or help you learn how to analyze stocks.

Then ask your broker to review and explain some of the resource materials you should use to analyze the stock he or she is recommending. Specifically, you'll need to become familiar with the Standard & Poor's and Value Line reports (see Figures 12.1 and 12.2 for an example of each). Standard & Poor's and Value Line analyze thousands of companies and publish revised reports on a regular basis. Here you'll recognize the language your broker speaks: betas, PE ratios, EPS, yield and so on. Armed with copies of the S&P reports and the Value Line for the stock your broker is recommending you study, ask him or her to point out the most important information in these reports—information a beginning investor must analyze when considering a stock for purchase. Your analysis of these reports will assist you in making your buy and sell decisions. Many helpful books for beginning investors are available.

## *Commission Fees*

Another important topic to discuss with your broker is the commission fees that your club will be charged on each stock transaction you make, whether you are buying or selling. This is how your broker earns a living; your broker and the brokerage firm each receive a percentage of these commission fees. Commissions are based on the stock's price and the number of shares involved in the transaction. Typically, stocks are purchased in increments of 100 shares, known as round lots. If your club purchases or sells fewer than 100 shares, called odd lots, the commission you are charged, as a percentage of the total cost of the trade, will be higher. These are illustrated in the following examples:

1. **Buy Round Lots**

   | | | |
   |---|---|---|
   | 100 shares of XYZ at $40 | = | $4,000 |
   | Plus commission charge | = | + 95 |
   | Total cost of trade | = | $4,095 |

Commission as a percentage of
trade = $95 ÷ $4,095                =     2.3%

2.  **Buy Odd Lots**

    25 shares of XYZ at $40            =   $1,000
    Plus commission charge             =   +   42
    Total cost of trade                =   $1,042

    Commission as a percentage of
    trade = 42 ÷ $1,042               =     4.0%

When you're ready to sell these shares, you will again be charged a commission, thus doubling your costs. Assume you want to sell your XYZ stock:

1.  **Sell Round Lots**

    100 shares of XYZ at $42           =   $4,200
    Subtract commission charge         =   -   95
    Total amount received              =   $4,105

2.  **Sell Odd Lots**

    25 shares of XYZ at $42            =   $1,050
    Subtract commission charge         =   -   42
    Total amount received              =   $1,008

These examples show the impact commission fees can have on your stock transactions. If you sell the 100 shares at $42, which is two points, or $2, above your purchase price of $40, you'll earn a grand total of $10 after commissions are paid. If you sell the 25 shares two points above your purchase price, you'll actually lose $34. Taking commission fees into account, the price of these 25 shares will have to increase to $43.50 just to break even.

1.  **Profits on Round Lots**

    Total amount received on sale of XYZ   =   $4,105
    Total amount paid to buy XYZ           =    4,095
    Total gain (loss) on sale of XYZ stock =   $    10

**FIGURE 12.1** Sample Standard & Poor's Stock Report

# Coca-Cola

562

**NYSE Symbol KO Options on CBOE (Feb-May-Aug-Nov) In S&P 500**

| Price | Range | P–E Ratio | Dividend | Yield | S&P Ranking | Beta |
|---|---|---|---|---|---|---|
| Oct. 21'94 | 1994 | | | | | |
| 50¼ | 51⅛–38⅞ | 26 | 0.78 | 1.6% | A+ | 1.00 |

## Summary

**Coca-Cola is the world's largest soft-drink company and has a sizable fruit juice business. Its bottling interests include 43% ownership of NYSE-listed Coca-Cola Enterprises. About 79% of 1993 operating profits came from international operations. Earnings are expected to continue in a strong uptrend through 1995, led by further aggressive worldwide expansion.**

## Current Outlook

**Earnings for 1995 are projected to rise to $2.30 a share, up from 1994's estimated $2.00.**

**The $0.19½ quarterly dividend is likely to be increased by approximately 15% in early 1995.**

Revenues should continue to advance at an approximately 10%-15% pace through 1995, driven principally by strong growth in worldwide unit case volume. Profit margins are expected to be sustained by the greater volume and, to a lesser degree, modest concentrate selling price increases and an improving geographic profit mix. Equity income should benefit from the greater volumes at bottlers. Reduced tax benefits on income generated in Puerto Rico will raise KO's effective tax rate in 1994 and beyond. Ongoing stock repurchases should contribute modestly to share earnings growth.

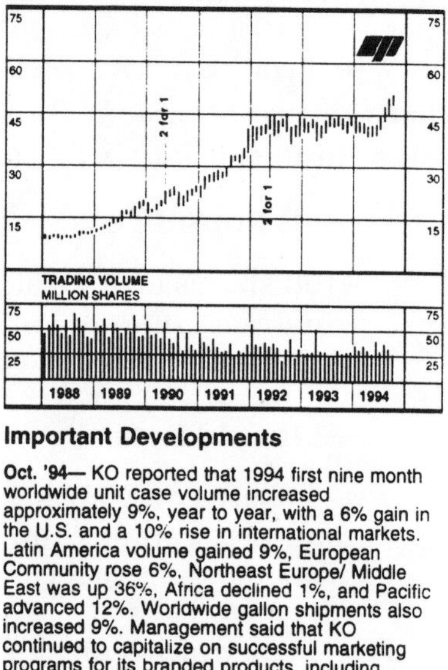


## Revenues (Billion $)

| Quarter: | 1994 | 1993 | 1992 | 1991 |
|---|---|---|---|---|
| Mar. | 3.35 | 3.06 | 2.77 | 2.48 |
| Jun. | 4.34 | 3.90 | 3.55 | 3.04 |
| Sep. | 4.46 | 3.63 | 3.51 | 3.17 |
| Dec. | --- | 3.37 | 3.24 | 2.88 |
| | --- | 13.96 | 13.07 | 11.57 |

Revenues for the nine months ended September 30, 1994 rose 15%, year to year, primarily reflecting increased soft drink gallon shipments. Margins were maintained, as lower expense ratios offset the consolidation of lower-margin bottling operations, and pretax profits advanced 16%. After taxes at 31.5% versus 31.3%, net income was up 15%, to $1.54 a share from $1.32, which was before a $0.01 charge for accounting changes.

## Common Share Earnings ($)

| Quarter: | 1994 | 1993 | 1992 | 1991 |
|---|---|---|---|---|
| Mar. | 0.40 | 0.35 | 0.29 | 0.24 |
| Jun. | 0.59 | 0.52 | 0.43 | 0.36 |
| Sep. | 0.55 | 0.45 | 0.41 | 0.34 |
| Dec. | E0.46 | 0.36 | 0.30 | 0.27 |
| | E2.00 | 1.68 | 1.43 | 1.21 |

## Important Developments

**Oct. '94**— KO reported that 1994 first nine month worldwide unit case volume increased approximately 9%, year to year, with a 6% gain in the U.S. and a 10% rise in international markets. Latin America volume gained 9%, European Community rose 6%, Northeast Europe/ Middle East was up 36%, Africa declined 1%, and Pacific advanced 12%. Worldwide gallon shipments also increased 9%. Management said that KO continued to capitalize on successful marketing programs for its branded products, including packaging initiatives, promotional programs and effective advertising. Separately, KO repurchased approximately 3 million shares of its common stock during 1994's third quarter, bringing the year-to-date total to approximately 13 million shares. Since January 1, 1984, KO has repurchased 27% of its outstanding common stock, or a cumulative 442 million shares.

**Next earnings report expected in early February.**

## Per Share Data ($)

| Yr. End Dec. 31 | 1993 | 1992 | 1991 | 1990 | [1]1989 | 1988 | [2]1987 | [2]1986 | 1985 | 1984 |
|---|---|---|---|---|---|---|---|---|---|---|
| Tangible Bk. Val. | **3.11** | 2.68 | 3.10 | 2.62 | 2.19 | 2.11 | 2.12 | 1.86 | 1.50 | 1.38 |
| Cash Flow | **1.94** | 1.67 | 1.41 | 1.20 | 0.98 | 0.83 | 0.71 | 0.88 | 0.65 | 0.51 |
| Earnings[3] | **1.68** | 1.43 | 1.21 | 1.02 | 0.85 | 0.72 | 0.61 | 0.61 | 0.43 | 0.40 |
| Dividends | **0.680** | 0.560 | 0.480 | 0.400 | 0.340 | 0.300 | 0.280 | 0.260 | 0.247 | 0.230 |
| Payout Ratio | **40%** | 39% | 39% | 39% | 39% | 41% | 46% | 43% | 56% | 57% |
| Prices—High | **45⅛** | 45⅜ | 40⅞ | 24½ | 20¼ | 11⁵⁄₁₆ | 13¼ | 11³⁄₁₆ | 7⅜ | 5½ |
| Low | **37½** | 35⁹⁄₁₆ | 21⅜ | 16⁵⁄₁₆ | 10¹³⁄₁₆ | 8¾ | 7 | 6⅜ | 4¹⁵⁄₁₆ | 4¹⁄₁₆ |
| P/E Ratio— | **27–22** | 32–25 | 34–18 | 24–16 | 24–13 | 16–12 | 22–12 | 19–11 | 17–12 | 14–10 |

Data as orig. reptd. Adj. for stk. divs. of 100% May 1992, 100% May 1990, 200% Jul. 1986. **1.** Refl. merger or acq. **2.** Refl. acctg. change. **3.** Bef. results of disc. ops. of +0.38 in 1989, +0.03 in 1985 & spec. item of -0.01 in 1993, -0.17 in 1992. E-Estimated.

Standard NYSE Stock Reports
Vol. 61/No. 210/Sec. 7

**October 31, 1994**



Standard & Poor's
25 Broadway, NY, NY 10004

Source: Reprinted by permission of Standard & Poor's, a division of McGraw-Hill, Inc.

**FIGURE 12.1**    (Continued)

## 562                                                    The Coca-Cola Company

### Income Data (Million $)

| Year Ended Dec. 31 | Revs. | Oper. Inc. | % Oper. Inc. of Revs. | Cap. Exp. | Depr. | Int. Exp. | [4]Net Bef. Taxes | Eff. Tax Rate | [5]Net Inc. | % Net Inc. of Revs. | Cash Flow |
|---|---|---|---|---|---|---|---|---|---|---|---|
| 1993 | 13,957 | 3,485 | 25.0 | 808 | 333 | 178 | 3,185 | 31.3% | [5]2,188 | 15.7 | 2,521 |
| 1992 | 13,074 | 3,080 | 23.6 | 1,083 | 310 | 171 | 2,746 | 31.4% | 1,884 | 14.4 | 2,194 |
| 1991 | 11,572 | 2,586 | 22.3 | 792 | 254 | 185 | 2,383 | 32.1% | 1,618 | 14.0 | 1,872 |
| 1990 | 10,236 | 2,237 | 21.9 | 642 | 236 | 231 | 2,014 | 31.4% | 1,382 | 13.5 | 1,600 |
| [1,2]1989 | 8,966 | 1,910 | 21.3 | 462 | 184 | 315 | 1,764 | 32.4% | 1,193 | 13.3 | 1,355 |
| 1988 | 8,338 | 1,768 | 21.2 | 387 | 170 | 239 | 1,582 | 34.0% | 1,045 | 12.5 | 1,208 |
| [3]1987 | 7,658 | 1,514 | 19.8 | 300 | 153 | 285 | 1,410 | 35.0% | [4]916 | 12.0 | 1,069 |
| [3]1986 | 8,669 | 1,755 | 20.2 | 373 | 430 | 208 | 1,511 | 38.2% | 934 | 10.8 | 1,364 |
| [1]1985 | 7,904 | 1,380 | 17.5 | 497 | 335 | 203 | 1,093 | 38.0% | 678 | 8.6 | 1,012 |
| 1984 | 7,364 | 1,227 | 16.7 | 396 | 170 | 150 | 1,068 | 41.1% | 629 | 8.5 | 798 |

### Balance Sheet Data (Million $)

| Dec. 31 | Cash | Assets | Curr. Liab. | Ratio | Total Assets | % Ret. on Assets | Long Term Debt | Common Equity | Total Cap. | % LT Debt of Cap. | % Ret. on Equity |
|---|---|---|---|---|---|---|---|---|---|---|---|
| 1993 | 1,078 | 4,434 | 5,171 | 0.9 | 12,021 | 19.0 | 1,428 | 4,584 | 6,125 | 23.3 | 51.8 |
| 1992 | 1,063 | 4,248 | 5,303 | 0.8 | 11,052 | 17.9 | 1,120 | 3,888 | 5,090 | 22.0 | 45.7 |
| 1991 | 1,117 | 4,144 | 4,118 | 1.0 | 10,222 | 16.6 | 985 | 4,426 | 5,611 | 17.6 | 39.6 |
| 1990 | 1,492 | 4,143 | 4,296 | 1.0 | 9,278 | 15.8 | 536 | 3,774 | 4,650 | 11.5 | 39.3 |
| 1989 | 1,182 | 3,604 | 3,658 | 1.0 | 8,283 | 15.5 | 549 | 3,185 | 4,330 | 12.7 | 38.5 |
| 1988 | 1,231 | 3,245 | 2,869 | 1.1 | 7,451 | 13.6 | 761 | 3,045 | 4,376 | 17.4 | 33.9 |
| 1987 | 1,468 | 4,136 | 4,119 | 1.0 | 8,356 | 11.1 | 803 | 3,224 | 4,237 | 19.0 | 27.7 |
| 1986 | 888 | 3,739 | 2,755 | 1.4 | 8,373 | 12.3 | 1,011 | 3,515 | 4,908 | 20.6 | 28.8 |
| 1985 | 865 | 2,970 | 2,004 | 1.5 | 6,898 | 10.6 | 889 | 2,979 | 4,189 | 21.2 | 23.7 |
| 1984 | 782 | 2,636 | 2,023 | 1.3 | 5,958 | 11.5 | 740 | 2,778 | 3,760 | 19.7 | 22.5 |

Data as orig. reptd.; finance subs. consol. after 1987. 1. Excl. disc. ops. 2. Refl. merger or acq. 3. Refl. acctg. change. 4. Incl. equity in earns. of nonconsol. subs. aft. 1982. 5. Bef. spec. item in 1992.

### Business Summary

Coca-Cola is the world's largest soft-drink company and a major producer of juice and related products. The company holds a 43% interest in Coca-Cola Enterprises, its largest bottler. Segment contributions in 1993:

| | Revs. | Profits |
|---|---|---|
| Soft drinks | 87% | 96% |
| Foods | 13% | 4% |

The company manufactures soft drink concentrates and syrups, which are sold to independent (and company-owned) bottlers and fountain wholesalers. Brands include Coca-Cola (best-selling soft drink in the world, including Coca-Cola classic), diet Coke (sold as Coke light in many territories outside the U.S.), Sprite, diet Sprite, Mr. PiBB, Mello Yello, Fanta, TAB, Fresca, PowerAde, Minute Maid soft drinks, and other products developed for specific markets, including Georgia brand coffee. Coca-Cola Nestle Refreshments, KO's 50% joint venture with Nestle S.A., produces ready-to-drink teas and coffees.

Coca-Cola Foods is the world's largest marketer and distributor of juice, juice drink, and related products. Brands include Minute Maid, Five Alive, Bright & Early, Hi-C, and Bacardi (under license).

International operations in 1993 accounted for 67% of net operating revenues (27% European Community; 21% Pacific & Canada; 12% Latin America; 5% Northeast Europe/Middle East; 2% Africa) and 79% of operating profits (29% Pacific & Canada; 25% European Community; 17% Latin America; 4% Northeast Europe/Middle East; 4% Africa).

Changes to U.S. tax law enacted in 1993 will limit the utilization of the favorable tax treatment from operations in Puerto Rico beginning in 1994, and will exert upward pressure on KO's effective tax rate.

### Dividend Data

Dividends have been paid since 1893. A dividend reinvestment plan is available.

| Amt. of Divd. $ | Date Decl. | Ex-divd. Date | Stock of Record | Payment Date |
|---|---|---|---|---|
| 0.19½ | Feb. 17 | Mar. 9 | Mar. 15 | Apr. 1'94 |
| 0.19½ | Apr. 21 | Jun. 9 | Jun. 15 | Jul. 1'94 |
| 0.19½ | Jul. 21 | Sep. 9 | Sep. 15 | Oct. 1'94 |
| 0.19½ | Oct. 20 | Nov. 25 | Dec. 1 | Dec. 15'94 |

### Capitalization

**Long Term Debt:** $1,471,000,000 (6/94).

**Common Stock:** 1,289,719,361 shs. ($0.25 par).
Berkshire Hathaway Inc. holds 7.3%.
Institutions hold 55%.
Shareholders of record: 179,165.

**Office—**1 Coca-Cola Plaza, N.W., Atlanta, GA 30313. **Tel—**(404) 676-2121. **Chrmn & CEO—**R. C. Goizueta. **Pres & COO—**M. D. Ivester. **VP & CFO—**J. L. Stahl. **Secy—**Susan E. Shaw. **Investor Contact—**Juan D. Johnson. **Dirs—**H. A. Allen, R. W. Allen, C. P. Black, W. E. Buffett, C. W. Duncan, Jr., R. C. Goizueta, S. B. King, D. F. McHenry, P. F. Oreffice, J. D. Robinson III, W. B. Turner, P. V. Ueberroth, J. B. Williams. **Transfer Agent & Registrar—**First Chicago Trust Co. of New York, NYC. **Incorporated** in Delaware in 1919. **Empl—**34,000.

Information has been obtained from sources believed to be reliable, but its accuracy and completeness are not guaranteed.    Kenneth A. Shea

**FIGURE 12.2    Sample Value Line Report**

| COCA-COLA NYSE-KO | RECENT PRICE 51 | P/E RATIO 24.9 (Trailing: 26.8 Median: 19.0) | RELATIVE P/E RATIO 1.72 | DIV'D YLD 1.5% | VALUE LINE 1535 |

TIMELINESS 1 Highest (Relative Price Performance Next 12 Mos.)
SAFETY 1 Highest
(Scale: 1 Highest to 5 Lowest)
BETA 1.10 (1.00 = Market)

1997-99 PROJECTIONS:

| | Price | Gain | Ann'l Total Return |
|---|---|---|---|
| High | 75 | (+45%) | 11% |
| Low | 65 | (+25%) | 8% |

Insider Decisions:

| | N | D | J | F | M | A | M | J | J |
|---|---|---|---|---|---|---|---|---|---|
| to Buy | 0 | 0 | 0 | 0 | 0 | 1 | 0 | 0 | 0 |
| Options | 0 | 4 | 0 | 0 | 0 | 2 | 5 | 0 | 0 |
| to Sell | 0 | 0 | 1 | 0 | 0 | 0 | 1 | 0 | 0 |

Institutional Decisions:

| | 3Q93 | 4Q93 | 1Q94 |
|---|---|---|---|
| to Buy | 229 | 210 | 213 |
| to Sell | 221 | 278 | 248 |
| Hld's(000) | 886091 | 898848 | 885864 |

Percent shares traded: 7.5 / 5.0 / 2.5

CAPITAL STRUCTURE as of 6/30/94
Total Debt $3472.0 mill.
LT Debt $1471.0 mill.  LT Interest $100.0 mill.
(Total interest coverage: 20x)    (22% of Cap'l)
Pension Liability None
Pfd Stock None
Common Stock 1,289,719,361 shs.
at July 29, 1994    (78% of Cap'l)

Options: CBOE
© VALUE LINE PUB., INC. 97-99

Target Price Range 1997 1998 1999

Relative Price Strength

10.5 x "Cash Flow" p sh

2-for-1 split

3-for-1 split

Shaded areas indicate recessions

| | 1978 | 1979 | 1980 | 1981 | 1982 | 1983 | 1984 | 1985 | 1986 | 1987 | 1988 | 1989 | 1990 | 1991 | 1992 | 1993 | 1994 | 1995 | 97-99 |
|---|---|---|---|---|---|---|---|---|---|---|---|---|---|---|---|---|---|---|---|
| Sales per sh A | 2.93 | 3.35 | 3.99 | 3.97 | 3.84 | 4.17 | 4.69 | 5.12 | 5.63 | 5.14 | 5.88 | 6.65 | 7.66 | 8.71 | 10.00 | 10.76 | 12.60 | 14.40 | 21.00 |
| "Cash Flow" per sh B | .32 | .36 | .37 | .40 | .41 | .44 | .51 | .55 | .63 | .72 | .85 | 1.01 | 1.20 | 1.41 | 1.69 | 1.96 | 2.30 | 2.65 | 4.00 |
| Earnings per sh B | .25 | .28 | .29 | .30 | .33 | .34 | .40 | .43 | .52 | .61 | .71 | .85 | 1.02 | 1.22 | 1.43 | 1.68 | 2.00 | 2.30 | 3.50 |
| Div'ds Decl'd per sh C | .15 | .16 | .18 | .19 | .21 | .22 | .23 | .25 | .26 | .28 | .30 | .34 | .40 | .48 | .56 | .68 | .78 | .88 | 1.10 |
| Cap'l Spending per sh | .21 | .22 | .19 | .21 | .20 | .23 | .22 | .26 | .24 | .20 | .27 | .34 | .44 | .60 | .83 | .82 | 1.00 | 1.10 | 1.70 |
| Book Value per sh D | 1.17 | 1.29 | 1.40 | 1.53 | 1.71 | 1.79 | 1.77 | 1.93 | 2.16 | 2.15 | 2.36 | 2.82 | 2.98 | 3.53 | 4.40 | 5.50 | | | 10.20 |
| Common Shs Outst'g E | 1482.3 | 1483.1 | 1483.5 | 1628.9 | 1636.2 | 1569.9 | 1543.9 | 1540.0 | 1489.4 | 1419.2 | 1348.1 | 1336.5 | 1329.0 | 1306.9 | 1297.5 | 1270.0 | 1250.0 | | 1190.0 |
| Avg Ann'l P/E Ratio | 13.7 | 11.4 | 9.7 | 9.6 | 12.6 | | 12.2 | 13.6 | 17.3 | 18.0 | 13.9 | 17.8 | 20.4 | 24.4 | 28.7 | 25.1 | | | 20.0 |
| Relative P/E Ratio | 1.87 | 1.65 | 1.29 | 1.17 | 1.07 | | 1.14 | 1.10 | 1.17 | 1.20 | 1.15 | 1.35 | 1.52 | 1.56 | 1.74 | 1.48 | | | 1.55 |
| Avg Ann'l Div'd Yield | 4.2% | 5.0% | 6.5% | 6.7% | 5.2% | | 4.8% | 4.2% | 2.9% | 2.6% | 3.0% | 2.3% | 1.9% | 1.6% | 1.4% | 1.6% | | | 1.5% |
| Sales ($mill) A | | | | | | 7364.0 | 7903.9 | 8668.6 | 7658.3 | 8337.8 | 8965.8 | 10236 | 11572 | 13074 | 13957 | 16000 | 18000 | | 25000 |
| Operating Margin | | | | | | 16.6% | 15.5% | 17.2% | 19.8% | 21.2% | 21.3% | 21.4% | 22.3% | 23.7% | 24.8% | 25.0% | 25.5% | | 25.5% |
| Depreciation ($mill) | | | | | | 166.1 | 178.1 | 166.8 | 153.5 | 169.8 | 183.8 | 243.9 | 261.4 | 321.9 | 360.0 | 380 | 410 | | 540 |
| Net Profit ($mill) | | | | | | 628.8 | 677.6 | 800.3 | 916.1 | 1044.7 | 1192.8 | 1381.9 | 1618.0 | 1883.8 | 2188.0 | 2560 | 2900 | | 4200 |
| Income Tax Rate | | | | | | 41.1% | 38.0% | 39.2% | 35.0% | 34.0% | 32.4% | 31.4% | 32.1% | 31.4% | 31.3% | 31.5% | 31.5% | | 31.5% |
| Net Profit Margin | | | | | | 8.5% | 8.6% | 9.2% | 12.0% | 12.5% | 13.3% | 13.5% | 14.0% | 14.4% | 15.7% | 16.0% | 16.1% | | 16.6% |
| Working Cap'l ($mill) | | | | | | 613.1 | 966.5 | 984.6 | 177 | 376.5 | d54.4 | d153.7 | d56.3 | d1056 | d737.0 | d635 | d590 | | d590 |
| Long-Term Debt ($mill) | | | | | | 740.0 | 889.2 | 1011.2 | 803.4 | 761.1 | 548.7 | 535.9 | 985.3 | 1120.1 | 1428.0 | 1440 | 1530 | | 1680 |
| Net Worth ($mill) | | | | | | 2778.1 | 2979.1 | 3515.0 | 3223.8 | 3345.3 | 3485.5 | 3849.2 | 4425.8 | 3888.4 | 4584.0 | 5600 | 6985 | | 12150 |
| % Earned Total Cap'l | | | | | | 18.9% | 18.7% | 18.8% | 23.8% | 28.2% | 30.2% | 32.2% | 30.6% | 38.4% | 37.7% | 36.5% | 35.0% | | 30.5% |
| % Earned Net Worth | | | | | | 22.6% | 22.7% | 22.8% | 28.4% | 31.2% | 34.2% | 35.9% | 36.6% | 48.4% | 47.7% | 45.5% | 42.5% | | 34.5% |
| % Retained to Comm Eq | | | | | | 9.5% | 9.7% | 11.3% | 15.3% | 19.8% | 22.0% | 22.0% | 22.1% | 29.5% | 28.5% | 27.0% | 26.0% | | 23.5% |
| % All Div'ds to Net Prof | | | | | | 58% | 57% | 50% | 45% | 42% | 41% | 40% | 40% | 39% | 40% | 39% | 38% | | 31% |

Bold figures are Value Line estimates

| CURRENT POSITION ($MILL.) | 1992 | 1993 | 6/30/94 |
|---|---|---|---|
| Cash Assets | 1063.0 | 1078.0 | 1356.0 |
| Receivables | 1055.2 | 1210.0 | 1534.0 |
| Inventory (Avg Cst) | 1018.6 | 1049.0 | 1166.0 |
| Other | 1110.9 | 1097.0 | 1237.0 |
| Current Assets | 4247.7 | 4434.0 | 5293.0 |
| Accts Payable | 2253.0 | 2217.0 | 2496.0 |
| Debt Due | 2087.3 | 1672.0 | 2001.0 |
| Other | 962.9 | 1282.0 | 1341.0 |
| Current Liab | 5303.2 | 5177.0 | 5838.0 |

| ANNUAL RATES of change (per sh) | Past 10 Yrs. | Past 5 Yrs. | Est'd '91-'93 to '97-'99 |
|---|---|---|---|
| Sales | 9.5% | 12.0% | 13.5% |
| "Cash Flow" | 15.0% | 18.0% | 15.5% |
| Earnings | 16.0% | 18.5% | 16.0% |
| Dividends | 10.5% | 15.5% | 11.5% |
| Book Value | 7.0% | 8.5% | 21.0% |

| Cal-endar | QUARTERLY SALES ($ mill.) Mar.31 | Jun.30 | Sep.30 | Dec.31 | Full Year |
|---|---|---|---|---|---|
| 1991 | 2481 | 3039 | 3173 | 2879 | 11572 |
| 1992 | 2772 | 3550 | 3508 | 3244 | 13074 |
| 1993 | 3056 | 3899 | 3629 | 3373 | 13957 |
| 1994 | 3352 | 4342 | 4461 | 3845 | 16000 |
| 1995 | 3750 | 4900 | 5000 | 4350 | 18000 |

| Cal-endar | EARNINGS PER SHARE Mar.31 | Jun.30 | Sep.30 | Dec.31 | Full Year |
|---|---|---|---|---|---|
| 1991 | .24 | .37 | .35 | .26 | 1.22 |
| 1992 | .29 | .43 | .41 | .30 | 1.43 |
| 1993 | .35 | .52 | .45 | .36 | 1.68 |
| 1994 | .40 | .59 | .55 | .46 | 2.00 |
| 1995 | .45 | .70 | .65 | .50 | 2.30 |

| Cal-endar | QUARTERLY DIVIDENDS PAID Mar.31 | Jun.30 | Sep.30 | Dec.31 | Full Year |
|---|---|---|---|---|---|
| 1990 | .10 | .10 | .10 | .10 | .40 |
| 1991 | .12 | .12 | .12 | .12 | .48 |
| 1992 | .14 | .14 | .14 | .14 | .56 |
| 1993 | .17 | .17 | .17 | .17 | .68 |
| 1994 | .195 | .195 | .195 | .195 | |

**BUSINESS:** The Coca-Cola Company is the world's largest soft drink company. Distributes major brands (Coca-Cola, Sprite, Fanta, TAB, etc.) through bottlers throughout the world. Foreign operations accounted for about 64% of net sales and 79% of profits in 1993. Food division, world's largest distributor of juice products (Minute Maid, Five Alive, Hi-C, etc.). Coca-Cola Enterprises, 44%-owned soft drink bottler. Advertising costs, 8.1% of sales. Has approximately 31,300 employees; 110,000 stockholders. Berkshire Hathaway owns 7.2% (1994 Proxy). 1993 depreciation rate: 6.4%. Estimated plant age: 5 years. Chairman and Chief Executive Officer: Roberto C. Goizueta. Incorporated: Delaware. Address: One Coca-Cola Plaza, Atlanta, Georgia 30313. Tel: 404-676-2121.

**Coca-Cola had a truly outstanding September quarter.** Worldwide unit case volume increased an impressive 13%, with the greatest strength, as expected, coming from outside North America, where total volume was up 17%. Total operating revenues were up an even larger 23%, aided by price increases and favorable foreign exchange rates. To be sure, conditions in the summer of 1993 had been particularly poor in both Europe and Japan, where wet and cold. But even so, we think that the numbers demonstrate the underlying growth potential of Coke's franchise, particularly outside the U.S.

**Business should be good again in 1995,** although we don't expect the gains to be as large as they were in the most recent quarter. Growth on the order of 4%-6% in the U.S. and 8%-10% elsewhere seems very achievable. Stronger economic conditions in Europe and Japan for the full year will help, and we look for continued good gains in newer markets, particularly in Eastern Europe, where demand has been extremely strong. **Prospects to 1997-99 look very promis-ing.** The company is only now completing the infrastructure necessary to begin to fully support growth in Eastern Europe. And starting from a very small base, Coke is likely to see solid growth there and in other largely untapped markets, including China and India. Meanwhile, there is also room for growth in more established markets where new types of packaging are making soft drinks more attractive.

**Coke shares now carry our number one rank for Timeliness.** That's because of the excellent recent earnings and the good stock performance. The issue, which had traded in a narrow range for nearly three years, has recently moved higher and is now about 15% above where it was three months ago. The appreciation potential to 3 to 5 years is somewhat below average, but given the company's well defined prospects, we still think the shares have appeal for conservative investors with a longer-term horizon. Coke shares will continue to be supported by the company's own aggressive stock repurchase program, which is scheduled to continue through the end of the decade.

*Stephen Sanborn, CFA November 18, 1994*

| | |
|---|---|
| Company's Financial Strength | A++ |
| Stock's Price Stability | 85 |
| Price Growth Persistence | 90 |
| Earnings Predictability | 100 |

To subscribe call 1-800-833-0046

(A) Includes Columbia Pictures: 7/82-12/86. Next earnings report due late Jan. Excludes special gains: '81, 44¢; '86, 17¢; also op. gain

(B) Based on average shares outstanding.

(loss) '83, (1¢); '85, 5¢; '89, 3¢; nonrec. gain (loss) '89, 73¢; '92, (17¢). (C) Next div'd meeting about Feb. 18. Goes ex about Mar. 9. Div'd payment dates: April 1, July 1, Oct. 1, Dec. 15.

(D) Incl. intangibles. In '93: $549.0 mill., 42¢/sh. (E) In millions, adjusted for stock splits. (F) Incl. only one payment. Another expected Dec. 15.

(G) Div'd reinvestment plan available.

Factual material is obtained from sources believed to be reliable, but the publisher is not responsible for any errors or omissions contained herein. For the confidential use of subscribers. Reprinting, copying, and distribution by permission only. Copyright 1994 by Value Line Publishing, Inc. ® Reg. TM—Value Line, Inc.

2. **Profits on Odd Lots**

Total amount received on sale of XYZ = $1,008
Total amount paid to buy XYZ = 1,042
Total gain (loss) on sale of XYZ stock = $( 34)

Ideally, all your trades should be in round lots (incre-ments of 100 shares), but that won't always be possible. For the first few years, when your portfolio is modest, you simply won't have adequate funds to purchase 100 shares of many stocks. For example, if you want to buy 100 shares of Coca-Cola today, it will cost you $5,400, not including the commission charge—a substantial amount of money. You have three alternatives, however:

1. You can purchase odd lots—less than 100 shares—re-alizing you'll pay a higher commission from a per-centage standpoint. But, if you've made a wise stock selection and intend to hold the stock for several years, its price should appreciate enough for you to realize a healthy profit after commissions are paid.
2. You can wait until you have accumulated enough funds to purchase round lots.
3. You can refer to Chapter 13, "Looking for Bargains," which suggests ways to lower your commission costs.

Ask your broker to hold all the stocks your club pur-chases. When your broker's firm holds your club's stocks under its name, that is called holding stocks in *street name.* Your broker then keeps a record of how many shares of each particular stock your club owns and reports this infor-mation to you on a monthly basis. This method of handling securities alleviates the burden of your membership having to care for individual stock certificates and makes trading much easier. If your club takes delivery of the actual stock certificates, these certificates should be kept in a safe de-posit box. This means one member of your club must make a trip to the safe deposit box whenever a trade is made.

## Select Industries To Study

Now that your broker has indicated the most important information you need to analyze on a S&P report and Value Line, and you've had some experience studying the stock your broker recommends, what is the next step? Start with a list of eight to ten industries you feel will perform well during the coming year or years. Here's where common sense is important. For example, we've all heard about the aging of America. Despite the fact that the drug stocks have been out of favor recently, it stands to reason that as our population ages, we'll need more pills to combat the aches and pains of growing old. And who will address our afflictions? Pharmaceutical companies.

Pass around a sign-up sheet, Figure 12.3, listing the industries you plan to study throughout the year and the month that members will present them at your meetings. Each member should volunteer to study several of the industries listed on the sheet. (This is where having an increased membership will ease the work load.) A month or so before an industry is to be presented, the two or three members who volunteered to study the industry to be presented should select two, three or four stocks within their industry to analyze and present at your meeting.

The sample sign-up sheet in Figure 12.3 shows the various industries to be presented, with space to write in your stock purchase decisions, which are made quarterly. This certainly is not cast in stone. You may decide to add to your portfolio every month. Since our investment contributions are modest, my club accumulates our contributions for three months, so that we have more money with which to buy stocks. You'll notice there is no industry presentation in December. That's the month when we clean up any unfinished business. Having sign-up sheets, however informal, encourages members to get involved in the study process and keeps your focus on learning how to invest in the stock market.

**FIGURE 12.3**    Sample Industry Sign-up Sheet

| | (Date) | |
|---|---|---|
| **Month** | **Industry** | **Member(s)** |
| January | Medical services | _____ |
| February | Drugstores | _____ |
| March | Manufactured housing | _____ |
| | Stock purchase decisions | _____ |
| April | Electronics | _____ |
| May | Chemicals | _____ |
| June | Metals and mining | _____ |
| | Stock purchase decisions | _____ |
| July | Computer software | _____ |
| August | Computers and peripherals | _____ |
| September | Semiconductors | _____ |
| | Stock purchase decisions | _____ |
| October | Beverage | _____ |
| November | Advertising | _____ |
| December | Stock purchase decisions | _____ |

Value Line has a section in the front of its book *Value Line Investment Survey* entitled "Timely Stocks in Timely Industries." Listed below are some of the industries Value Line anticipates will perform well during 1995:

| | |
|---|---|
| Advertising | Drugstores |
| Beverage | Electronics |
| Chemicals | Medical Services |
| Computers and Peripherals | Metals and Mining |
| Computer Software | Semiconductors |

Value Line also lists the five or six stocks it expects to perform well within each industry. Now you have a starting point. Let's assume your membership wants to research the beverage industry. Using the S&P or Value Line stock report, the two or three volunteers responsible for this industry could analyze Coca-Cola, PepsiCo and one or two other stocks, compare their information using the stock study worksheet discussed later in this chapter and present their purchase recommendations to your membership. Also, don't be afraid to ask your club's broker to suggest stocks to analyze. After all, information and assistance are two of the reasons you're doing business with him or her.

The Standard & Poor's and Value Line reports, like those examples in Figures 12.1 and 12.2, are available to individuals, but they are expensive and quite cumbersome. Your broker should make these reports available to you, and your local library also may have copies you can use.

My club's broker has shown us where her firm keeps its Value Line reports and how to operate the copy machine. We simply help ourselves to the *Value Line Investment Survey* and make copies of the individual stock reports. The brokerage firm also is quick to provide computer printouts of any S&P reports we request.

Standard & Poor's provides informational reports on more than 7,500 companies. These reports are revised whenever a company issues new information that will have an impact on its stock. Value Line tracks 1700 stocks and publishes quarterly updates on each stock in its *Value Line Investment Survey.* Standard & Poor's provides brokerage firms with computer access to their reports which will enable you to receive up-to-the-minute information on companies you wish to analyze.

Both Standard & Poor's and Value Line have a ranking system for the stocks they analyze. Value Line includes a ranking system for timeliness and safety, with 1 being the highest and 5 the lowest. Standard & Poor's includes the star ranking system in their computer printouts: *****, buy; ****, accumulate; ***, average performer—not recommended for purchase; **, avoid; and *, sell. Both reports are extremely detailed. Don't get discouraged. It will take time to become familiar with all the information they contain.

## Look around You

The industry approach is one of several good ways to start researching stocks. But pay attention to your surroundings—the clothes you wear, the food you eat, where you do your shopping. Don't limit yourselves solely to choosing stocks within preselected industries. You can find lots of stocks to research that may not fit into your industry classifications but ones that you would do well to own.

For example, most of the women in my club try to do it all—they work, keep house, chauffeur the children and help with their school activities. One of our members remarked how good and convenient Healthy Choice frozen dinners are. We had no plans to study the food industry, but because of this endorsement, we analyzed ConAgra, the manufacturer of this product, and purchased 100 shares of its stock. ConAgra became a real success story for us—the stock's price appreciated 50 percent in one year!

Another example of paying attention to your surroundings and a great success story for us is the Gap. Three of my club's members recently became grandmothers. Nothing is more fun than shopping for a new grandchild, and these new grandmothers discovered the Baby Gap. After hearing our members rave about the Gap's baby and kids' clothes, we bought 100 shares of the Gap at $28.25 and sold the stock for $42.75 less than a year later. Peter Lynch, author of *Beating the Street* and *One Up on Wall Street*, is a real believer in investing in a company you understand; this advice certainly worked in our case.

Current investment books, magazines and newspapers provide a wealth of investment ideas. In addition, most brokerage firms have their own in-house publications that suggest stocks to analyze.

## Develop a Stock Study Worksheet

Figure 12.4 shows a sample worksheet for beginning investors. This sheet is extremely basic and includes some of the important data that your broker most likely recommended for you to analyze. The committee studying a particular industry for the month should prepare these worksheets and distribute them to each club member when the stock is presented. Stock study worksheets will help your members decide whether to buy one of the stocks under consideration. Pay particular attention to the section asking for your reasons to purchase the stock. List good reasons for buying the stock—a hot tip won't do. You'll need to review these reasons periodically to determine whether they're still valid. As your members gain investment expertise, revise the worksheet to reflect your expanded investment knowledge. Also, the NAIC has developed special stock study guides to help you analyze prospective stocks for purchase.

## Initiate a Stock Purchase Schedule

In Chapter 3, "Uncovering the Ingredients of Success," I stressed the importance of investing on a regular basis. If your monthly investment contributions are modest, consider purchasing stocks on a quarterly basis. Continue to study different stocks each month and deposit your investment contributions into your club's interest-bearing money market account. Then, at the end of each quarter, you will have accumulated three months' worth of contributions with which to buy stocks.

**FIGURE 12.4**    Sample Stock Study Worksheet

Date prepared: ___December 29, 1994___

Stock Name:    Coca-Cola            Symbol: · KO

Business Description: World's largest soft drink company (Coca-Cola, Sprite, Fanta, TAB), and world's largest distributor of juice products (Minute Maid, Five Alive, Hi-C).

Current Price: ___$52.25___            Stock Exchange: ___NYSE___

52-Week High: ___$53.50___            Low: ___$38.87___

Current P/E: ___24.9___            Average Industry P/E: ___24___

Average P/E over last 4 years: ___23.28___

Timeliness: ___1___            Safety: ___1___

Annual Dividend: ___$0.78___            Yield: ___1.5%___

Company's Financial Strength: ___A++ per Value Line___

Long-Term Debt: ___22%___            BETA: ___1.10___

Percent held by Institutional Investors: ___55%___

Industry Outlook: ___Gains look particularly favorable in Eastern Europe, but industry should also do well in China and India.___

**Financial Highlights:**

1. Have sales/revenues increased steadily over past 4 years? If not, why?
   Yes, average gain of 12 percent per year
2. Have earnings increased steadily over past 4 years? If not, why?
   Yes, average increase of 18 percent per year
3. Has book value per share increased steadily over past 4 years? If not, why?
   Yes, average increase of 9.8 percent per year
4. 1997–1999 Projections:            High: ___$75.00___    Low: ___$65.00___
5. Are sales and earnings projected to increase 1997–1999? If so, how much?
   Sales: 45.8% increase; EPS: 52.1% increase

**Comments:**

A strong company for conservative investors with a longer-term investment horizon.

**Reasons to purchase stock:**

Company's stock repurchase program
Company now completing infrastructure to begin to support growth in Eastern Europe
New packaging making soft drinks more attractive
Company's financial strength
Value Line's ranking for timeliness and safety
S&P's high recommendation
International growth predicted at 7 percent to 10 percent a year for the next several years

Action Taken:            Date: ___January 15, 1995___

_____ Voted to hold for further consideration.

___14___ Voted to purchase ___25___ shares @ ___market___ /share.

___1___ Voted not to purchase this stock.

Member responsible for following stock: ___Susan___

For example, let's say that in January, two members present three stocks in the medical services industry with accompanying stock study worksheets, which all members have reviewed and discussed. One member then makes a motion, based on the medical services committee's recommendations, to hold one of the stocks in that industry for purchase consideration at the end of the quarter. You follow this format in February and March, asking the responsible members to research and present stocks in the industries listed on the industry sign-up sheet (Figure 12.3). At the end of the quarter, you'll make your buy decisions from the various stocks you've studied and held for consideration during the past three months. Of course, you'll have to decide whether to buy a few shares of several stocks or more shares of one stock. Remember, though, brokerage fees are based on round lot purchases, and you'll pay a higher commission fee, percentage-wise, on fewer than 100 shares.

Even though some members will own more units of the club than others, your buy and sell decisions should be passed by a simple majority of the members, provided you have a quorum present.

## Assign Members Responsibility for Tracking Stocks

The last line of the stock study worksheet in Figure 12.4 asks for the name of the member responsible for a particular stock in your club's portfolio. Usually, one member of the study committee that presented the stock will volunteer to be responsible. That member must follow the stock and report relevant information appearing in the newspapers, investment magazines, television news programs and updated S&P and Value Line reports. The responsible member should also keep a record of the committee's stock study worksheet and update it periodically. Generally, this is the member who makes buy or sell recommendations to the entire club on the stock he or she is following. Consider rotating member responsibility every year so that other club members have an opportunity to become familiar with more than one stock in your club's portfolio.

## Fidelity Bond

A fidelity bond is a form of insurance policy that holds your investment club harmless from any losses that may result through dishonesty or negligence on the part of those officers who handle the club's funds and who are identified in the bond. If your club incurs any losses through dishonesty or negligence of the insured officers, it will be reimbursed up to the amount of the bond.

As the assets of your club's portfolio increase, don't be surprised if your accountant or attorney suggests that you purchase a fidelity bond for your treasurer. It makes good business sense to protect against the conversion of assets for personal use. The NAIC offers this type of coverage to investment clubs at a reasonable rate, provided that the club adheres to required NAIC guidelines. Your independent insurance agent also can help you secure a fidelity bond. Typically, coverage is for one year and it is renewable every year. The cost of the premium depends on the amount of the club's assets and the number of members being insured.

One of the keys to building a solid portfolio is to do your homework before you begin to invest. Because you should address so many details before you enter the market, it's a good idea to follow Figure 12.5, a checklist summarizing all the subjects that you should discuss with your broker, as well as listing the other investment procedures key to becoming successful stock market investors.

**FIGURE 12.5**    Investment Procedures Checklist

# Investment Procedures

## ✓ CHECKLIST

☐    1.  Seek Broker Assistance

    ☐    A.  Review of in-house publications

    ☐    B.  Review Standard & Poors and Value Lines

    ☐    C.  Learn/understand important information for stock analyses

    ☐    D.  Arrange to use brokerage firm's copy machine

    ☐    E.  Discuss stocks being held in street name and review brokerage firm's monthly reports

    ☐    F.  Discuss commission fees

    ☐    G . Discuss round lot versus odd lot purchases relative to commission fees

☐    2.  Select Industries to Study

☐    3.  Develop a Stock Study Worksheet

☐    4.  Initiate a Stock Purchase Schedule

☐    5.  Begin Investing

# Tips for Success

DRIP Is a Beautiful Sound

Pay Attention to Details

Dollar Cost Averaging Makes Sense

CHAPTER 13

# LOOKING FOR
# BARGAINS

*I*nvestment clubs, because of their nature, often are slow to react. A lot can happen in the stock market from one meeting to the next, and there's a good chance you'll miss some golden opportunities. Of course, your membership can set up a telephone hotline to make important buy and sell decisions, but that seems cumbersome. Besides, by the time you reach one-half of your members to seek their approval for action, it will probably be too late. This chapter presents some methods of trading, buying and selling stocks, that are appropriate for investment clubs. Since you will need time to become familiar with these techniques, Figure 13.1 highlights the important points of each trading method discussed.

# Trading Techniques

## *Market Order*

Let's assume your club met last night and discussed purchasing stock in XYZ company, which has been trading at
between 40 and 40½ for the past few days. Your membership passed a motion to buy 50 shares of XYZ company
at market and instructed your treasurer to place the order
with your broker. Today, when your order reaches the
trading floor, it will be executed at the prevailing market
price. You also can use this technique to sell shares you
own, and it couldn't be easier.

## *Good 'Til Canceled Order versus Day Order*

Now, let's assume your club met last night and passed a
motion to buy 50 shares of XYZ company; however, because of the market's volatility and a weakness in the
economy, you think that between now and next month's
club meeting, there's a good chance that these shares will
trade below today's market price of 40½. Your membership
instructed your treasurer to place a good 'til canceled (GTC)
order with your broker for 50 shares at, say, 35. This GTC
order means that if and when XYZ's price drops to 35, your
order will be executed and you will have saved yourselves
some money. How long good 'til canceled orders remain in
effect varies from brokerage firm to brokerage firm. At
some firms these orders last indefinitely; at other firms,
they last 30 days. If you do not specify a GTC order, your
broker will assume you are placing a day order. A day order
is in effect only for one day, which means it either will be
executed or will expire at the end of the day it is placed. You
will not be charged a fee for placing either of these orders.
However, you will be charged the normal brokerage commission if or when they are executed.

### Discount Brokers

A discount broker could accomplish both of the above trades. I don't recommend using discount brokers; however, until your membership has a good understanding of the stock market and doesn't need to tap the investment knowledge or services a full service broker provides. Of course, discount brokers aren't free. Their fees, too, are based upon the price of the stock and number of shares traded. Only you can decide whether the additional commission fees you pay your full service broker are worth the extra benefits you receive.

### Dividend Reinvestment Plans (DRIPs)

Several months have passed, and XYZ company's earnings prospects look even better than you anticipated. You would do well to consider buying more shares. Unfortunately, your club doesn't have enough money in its treasury to purchase another 50 shares, and as the illustration in Chapter 12 showed, the commission charge on a purchase of 25 shares, as a percent of the trade, will be extremely high. The good news is that XYZ's Value Line report indicates the company has a dividend reinvestment plan (DRIP). Ask your broker to transfer XYZ's stock from street name to your club's name so you can participate in the plan. (Many brokerage firms now charge a fee for this service.) You'll also need to contact the reinvestment plan's "transfer agent" for an enrollment card, assuming your club meets the plan's minimum share requirement. You can contact the plan's agent through the company at the address or telephone number indicated on the Value Line or Standard & Poor's report. Once enrolled, the dividends you would normally receive from the company will be used to purchase additional shares of stock. You also may send a specific dollar amount, say $100 each month, to the company to buy more shares. It's a painless way to purchase stock, because you don't have to worry about market timing or brokerage commissions.

## A Low-Cost Investment Plan

The NAIC has gone one step further in making stock affordable to its members. It has solicited the participation of a number of companies (that number is always growing) in its low-cost investment plan. If your investment club joins the NAIC, it can purchase one share of XYZ stock from the NAIC by sending enough money to cover the cost of this one share, plus an additional $15 to cover price fluctuation and the service fee. The NAIC will then deposit your money in an escrow account until XYZ's established monthly investment date. At that time, the NAIC will send your money, along with other investors', to the administrator of XYZ company's reinvestment plan. After the NAIC has purchased the stock, it will advise XYZ company's stock transfer agent to transfer the proper number of shares out of the NAIC's account and into an account in the name of your investment club. Once this is accomplished, you'll send all future payments to XYZ company directly. To learn more about this plan and receive a list of the participating companies, contact the NAIC at the following address: PO Box 220, Royal Oak, MI 48068; 810-583-6242.

## Selling Shares in a Dividend Reinvestment Plan

You have two ways to sell the shares you hold in a dividend reinvestment plan:

1.  You may contact the dividend paying agent who is responsible for keeping dividend records and ask the agent to liquidate your shares. You may be charged a liquidation fee for this service. This will be done at a time (usually once a month) and price (the prevailing market price at the time of liquidation) determined by the agent.

2.  You can ask the dividend paying agent to send your club the actual stock certificates for the full shares it owns.

Once you have these certificates, give them to your broker for safe keeping. Then, when you want to sell these shares, it's simply a matter of endorsing the certificates over to your broker and placing a market order to sell. Of course, you'll have to pay the normal commission fee if your broker executes your order. The dividend paying agent won't send stock certificates for any fractional shares your club may own, but will liquidate these shares and send your club a check, along with a stock certificate for the full shares you own.

## Dollar Cost Averaging

With this simple trading strategy, you send a specific amount of money, at regular intervals, to a company whose stock you wish to own. This is a disciplined approach to investing; you won't have to worry about market timing (when is a good time to buy into the market), and you won't have to pay commission fees. Enrollment in a company's dividend reinvestment plan or the NAIC's Low-Cost Investment Plan allows your club to dollar cost average, a cost-effective way to accumulate additional shares of stock.

Even though you send the same amount of money each month, your dollars will purchase more shares when the market is down and fewer shares when the market is up. Let's suppose that your club sends $100 each month to XYZ company:

| | |
|---|---|
| XYZ stock @ $50 per share—January | 2.000 shares |
| XYZ stock @ $45 per share—February | 2.222 shares |
| XYZ stock @ $43 per share—March | 2.326 shares |
| XYZ stock @ $48 per share—April | 2.083 shares |
| **Total** | 8.631 |

So, if your club invested a total of $400 and owned a total of 8.631 shares, the average cost per would be $46.34 per share:

$$\frac{\$400.00}{8.631\ \text{shares}} = \$46.34\ \text{per share}$$

My investment club wanted to own a particular bank stock, but we couldn't afford to purchase 100 shares all at once. Instead, we bought 10 shares of the stock and joined the company's dividend reinvestment plan. We then passed a motion to send $100 every month to the company to purchase additional shares. This method of buying stock should be viewed as a long-term approach to investing, and it works particularly well with high-quality growth stocks.

## Stop Loss Orders

Buying stock is fun, but selling stock is even more fun, provided that you stand to make a profit. Let's assume the XYZ stock you bought from your broker at 35 is now trading at 50—a gain of more than 40 percent! You can employ a technique to protect this profit or (perish the thought) limit a loss.

Susan Bondy, a syndicated financial columnist and author of *How To Make Money Using Other People's Money*, recommends placing stop loss orders on all the stocks you own; that is, setting a price at which your stocks will automatically be sold. She suggests setting sell order prices on conservative, blue chip stocks at 10 percent below your purchase price; 15 percent below your purchase price for stocks of moderate risk or long-term growth stocks; and 20 percent below for high-risk stocks and those on the Nasdaq. Then, as your stocks begin to move upward, adjust your stop loss orders to reflect these movements. For example, when you purchased XYZ, a long-term growth stock, at 35, you would have placed a stop loss order at 29¾ or 15 percent below your purchase price. Today, XYZ's stock is selling at 50, but has gone as high as 51. Adjust your stop order to 43½, which is approximately 15 percent below its high of 51.

Stop loss orders should be directly related to a stock's volatility. The more volatile the stock, the more movement you should allow in setting a stop loss price. Because of market volatility and the amount of time it takes investment clubs to react, this is a good technique to protect your gains or cap your losses. Also, sometimes it seems easier for investment clubs to do "nothing" rather than "something," so stop loss orders act as a form of insurance for action. Like good until canceled orders and day orders, you will not be charged a fee for placing these stop loss orders. You will be charged the normal commission fee, however, if and when your stop loss order is executed.

These stop loss orders are placed with your broker, who enters them into a computer. When the stock's price falls to your figure, your order becomes a market order to sell, and the sale is made as close to your price as possible. You cannot place stop loss orders on shares held in a dividend reinvestment plan, however. And stop loss orders have their drawbacks in today's volatile market. Sometimes negative news will come out on a stock after the market closes for the day. When the market opens the following morning, the stock's price may have fallen three or four points below your stop figure and your order will be executed. Then, a few hours later after the hoopla has died down, the stock's price will be back where it was the previous day. About all you've done in this scenario is lose money yourself and make money for your broker. So before you use this strategy, talk to your broker to be certain you understand how these stop orders work and the pitfalls involved.

Part III of the full financial report illustrated in Chapter 8 (Figure 8.1) included a "stop loss" column. This column should indicate any stop loss orders you have placed. It's easy to forget the actual dollar amount of your order, so in-

**FIGURE 13.1**   Summary of Trading Techniques

**Market Order To Buy/Sell**

Placed with your broker on a specific stock at the prevailing market price. You will be charged a commission on the trade.

**Good 'Til Canceled Order To Buy/Sell**

Placed with your broker on a specific stock at a specific price. Your order is good until you cancel it. (Confirm time limit with broker.) Your order will be executed only when the stock's price reaches your order figure. You will be charged a commission if the trade is made.

**Day Order**

Same as above, but the order is in effect only for one day— the day it is placed.

**Dividend Reinvestment Plans**

**Company Plan**

You must first own stock in the company. Then, contact the company to enroll using the phone number shown on Value Line and S&P. Once enrolled, all dividends will automatically be used to buy more shares of the company's stock. You may also make voluntary contributions at any time to purchase additional shares, and you will not be charged a commission. When you sell, you will not be charged a commission if you liquidate your shares through the plan. If you request the actual stock certificates and you sell the shares through your broker, you will pay a commission. You will receive certificates only for the full shares you own; fractional shares will be liquidated through the plan

**NAIC's Low-Cost Investment Plan**

This plan allows you to make your initial stock purchase through the NAIC, thus avoiding a brokerage commission. After the NAIC purchases the shares you have ordered, the stock is transferred to an account established in your club's name. You then become a member of the company's plan and send all future contributions to the company, not the NAIC. You must be a member of the NAIC to participate in this plan.

**FIGURE 13.1**   (Continued)

### Dollar Cost Averaging

By buying a company's stock at regular intervals (through a reinvestment plan or your broker), you can lower your total per share cost of the stock. To determine the average cost per share, divide the number of shares owned by the total amount invested. Example: Buy one share at $1 and, later, buy one share at $2. You would then own two shares at an average cost of $1.50 per share.

### Stop Loss Orders

A strategy used to protect gains or cap losses whereby you place a good until canceled order with your broker to sell your stock at a specified price. The price you specify should be a percentage figure (e.g. 10%, 15%, 20%) *below* your purchase price. You should raise your stop order as the stock's price rises. You cannot use this strategy on stocks held in a dividend reinvestment plan. You will pay a commission if your order is executed.

### Limit Order

Similar to stop loss orders, but limit orders are executed only if the stock's price stays at or goes higher after it touches your sell order price. You cannot use this strategy on stocks held in a reinvestment plan, and you will pay a commission if your order is executed.

clude the stop figure in your reports as a reminder to check your orders against the stocks' current prices.

## Limit Order

Another selling technique you can use is a limit order, which is an order to buy a stock at a specified price or lower or to sell a stock at a specified price or higher. To illustrate the difference between a stop loss order and a limit order, let's assume that you bought XYZ company's stock at 35 and you placed a stop loss order on XYZ at 43½. As soon as

XYZ's stock touches your 43½ figure, your stop loss order will become a market order to sell, and your stock will be executed at the next available price, whether XYZ's price is 44, 43½ or 42⅞. If you place a limit order at 43½, your order also will be triggered as soon as the stock's price touches your 43½ figure; however, your order will be executed only if your stock stays at your limit order of 43½ or goes higher.

Investors become unhappy with stop loss orders because in a rapidly declining market, they may not get the price they've ordered for their stock—it may be a fraction or so less. But suppose you had placed a limit order on XYZ at 43½ and trading was suspended for the day. Then when trading resumed the following morning, XYZ's stock price was 40—well below your limit sell price of 43½. What would happen? Your order would not be executed, and you would still own the stock. There is no general rule for setting limit orders. However, when they first buy a stock, many traders make a practice of setting a limit order that will return a 20 percent profit on their investment.

No one trading technique is better than another—all have merit. Most likely, you'll use all the buying and selling methods I've presented depending upon how much money you have available, how badly you want to own or liquidate a particular stock or how quickly you want to accomplish the trade.

## Keeping a Record of Your Transactions

Once you begin buying and selling stock, your treasurer should keep a record, by company, of every stock transaction you make. This means keeping track of every dollar you invest and every share of stock you receive, whether through simple market orders placed with your broker or through dividend reinvestment plans.

Figure 13.2 illustrates the transactions that have occurred with XYZ company: The first line indicates the $5 fee you paid to participate in XYZ's dividend reinvestment plan. The second line reflects your first investment of $110, which resulted in the purchase of 2.200 shares at a price of $50 per share. The third line indicates that in February you sent an additional $100 and purchased 2.222 shares at $45, bringing your total shares owned to 4.422. Also in February, you reinvested a $0.45 dividend and received an additional 0.010 share of XYZ stock. Continuing with this illustration, you invested $100 in March and again in April, bringing your total net invested to $410.45, for which you received 8.841 shares of stock. This results in an average price per share of $46.43—dollar cost averaging at work! Below these figures you will see a record of the sale of your XYZ stock. In this example, you received a per share price of $53.50 for your stock. Subtracting your liquidation fee, you enjoyed a gain of $61.07 or 14.9 percent on your original investment. These records are an important part of your club's investment history; make sure to update them whenever a transaction occurs that affects the stock.

**FIGURE 13.2**    Sample Stock Transaction Record

## XYZ COMPANY

| Transaction | Date | Purchase Price Share | Cash Invested | Reinvested Dividend | Net Invested | Number of Shares Bought | Number of Shares Dividend Reinvested | Total Shares Owned |
|---|---|---|---|---|---|---|---|---|
| FEE | | | $ 5.00 | | | | | 2.200 |
| Beginning Purchase | 1/2/92 | $50.00 | $110.00 | | $110.00 | 2.200 | | 4.422 |
| Cash Invested | 2/15/92 | $45.00 | $100.00 | | $100.00 | 2.222 | | 4.432 |
| Reinvested Dividend | 2/25/92 | $45.00 | | $0.45 | $ 0.45 | | 0.010 | 6.758 |
| Cash Invested | 3/15/92 | $43.50 | $100.00 | | $100.00 | 2.326 | | 8.841 |
| Cash Invested | 4/15/92 | $48.00 | $100.00 | | $100.00 | 2.083 | | 8.841* |
| TOTAL | | | $415.00 | $0.45 | $410.45 | 8.831 | 0.010 | |

$410.54 ÷ 8.841 = $46.43 Cost per share

## Sale

| Transaction | Date | Number of Shares | Share Price | Commission | Total Received | Net Invested | Gain/ Loss | % Gain/ Loss |
|---|---|---|---|---|---|---|---|---|
| | 6/30/92 | 8.841 | $53.50 | $1.47 | $471.52 | $410.45 | $61.07 | 14.9 |

# Epilogue

# Food for Thought

*U*ndertake something that is difficult;
it will do you good.
Unless you try to do something beyond
what you have already mastered,
you will never grow.

*Ronald E. Osborn*

*W*e have had quite a walk down Wall Street! The learning process is never easy and it's never over. We usually take one step forward and two back. My club's first two stock purchases are a good example: We bought Wendy's for $16 per share and Perry Drug for $17. When we sold these stocks two years later, Wendy's price was $6.88 and Perry Drug's was $7.50, both down more than 50 percent. But that's why the investment club approach is such a good one. It's likely that your contributions are modest, so the amount you might lose in a market correction or poor stock selection won't be disastrous. Turn your negatives into positives—consider a mistake the cost of a concept well learned. Thomas Edison said that he never had any failures, just learning experiences. And Malcolm Forbes said, "Failure is success if we learn from it." You may not win a million dollars in the lottery, but your investment club experience will pay even greater dividends: Pride in the knowledge you gain and pleasure in the friendships you make.

APPENDIX *A*

# ARTICLES OF ASSOCIATION

*Before you file the necessary legal documents to become a business, you should consult a lawyer and an accountant to be sure you meet the laws of the state in which you are forming your investment club and that you understand the tax consequences involved.*

1. **Formation of Association.** The undersigned hereby form a cooperative association in accordance with the law of the State of _____ . The name of the association shall be _____ . The association is formed for the purpose of educating its members in securities evaluation and for investment through periodic contributions by the members for their mutual benefit.

2. **Term.** The association shall commence on the date these Articles of Association are executed by the founding members and shall continue for a time not limited by these Articles until dissolved as hereinafter provided.

3. **Meetings.** The members of the association shall meet not less frequently than monthly, at times and places to be determined by the membership.

4. **Contributions.** Each member shall be required to make a monthly contribution to the association in an amount to be determined by a majority vote of the members.

5. **Officers.** At the initial meeting of the members, they shall elect officers of the association as follows:

a. A *president,* who shall preside at all meetings and shall serve as the chief executive officer of the association.

b. A *vice president,* who shall perform the duties of president in the absence or incapacity of the president.

c. A *secretary,* who shall have custody of and maintain the records of the association and shall prepare and maintain written minutes of meetings and decisions taken by the membership.

d. A *treasurer,* who shall establish and maintain in the name of the association necessary bank depository accounts and shall make monthly reports to the members as to the financial condition of the association. The association by resolution may designate one or more officers, in addition to the treasurer, who may withdraw funds from the association bank accounts. The treasurer shall maintain written accounts of the transactions of the association, which shall at all reasonable times be available to any member for examination. Not less than annually, the treasurer shall furnish to each member a full and complete written accounting of the assets and liabilities of the association, and of the capital accounts of each member.

In addition to the above enumerated duties, the officers shall perform such other duties as are commonly associated with their offices or as directed by resolution of the members.

The officers shall serve for such terms as may be prescribed by resolution of the membership and until their successors are duly elected and qualified. The members by resolution may require a fidelity bond be secured at association expense covering the fidelity of any officer. Any officer may be removed by a two-thirds vote of the entire membership during his or her term of office for neglect of his or her responsibilities or for malfeasance in office.

6. **Securities Broker.** The members of the association shall by resolution select a securities broker to execute orders placed by the authorized officers of the association. The broker shall not be a member of the association. The members by appropriate resolution shall designate the officer or officers of the association authorized to purchase or sell securities through the

broker, and the broker may rely upon such resolution until it is modified, changed or rescinded in writing. Stocks, bonds and securities owned by the association shall be registered in the association name, or in the names of one or more officers as trustees for the association, or may be left with the broker to be held in the "street name" for the account of the association. Any corporation or transfer agent called upon to transfer securities to or from the name of the association or a trustee for the association may rely upon instructions or assignments signed by a designated officer or officers of the association.

7. **Compensation.** No officer or other member shall be compensated for services rendered to the association; however, reasonable and necessary association expenses shall be reimbursed by the association.

8. **New Members.** Additional members may be admitted at any time by unanimous consent of all members. As a condition of membership, all members agree to be bound by the terms of these Articles of Association and by all resolutions adopted or to be adopted by vote of the members.

9. **Withdrawal of Members.** A member may withdraw from the association at any time. Death or legal incapacity of a member shall be handled in the same manner as a voluntary withdrawal. A withdrawing member shall give written notice to the association's secretary or any other officer. The effective date of such withdrawal shall be as of the next regularly scheduled association meeting. The date for valuation of the withdrawing member's interest shall be the first regular meeting following the meeting at which notice of withdrawal is received. Between receipt of the notice of withdrawal and the subsequent withdrawal valuation date, the other members shall have the option to purchase, in proportion to their capital account in the association, the capital account of the withdrawing member. If the other members do not elect to purchase the capital account of the withdrawing member by such valuation date, the association shall use cash on hand or sell sufficient securities to pay the withdrawing member the value of his or her capital account, less the actual cost of selling sufficient securities to obtain the cash necessary to meet the withdrawal. The withdrawing member shall be paid in cash, but without interest, not later than ninety (90) days after such valuation date.

10. **Nonassignability of Member's Interest.** No member may assign, transfer, pledge or hypothecate his or her membership or capital account, in whole or in part, and any attempt to do so shall be construed as such member's election to withdraw from the association.

11. **Quorum, Amendment of Articles and Dissolution.** A quorum for the transaction of business shall be two-thirds of the membership of the association, and the election of officers and the transaction of other business shall be by a majority of the members present and voting, providing a quorum is present. These Articles of Association may be amended or the association may be dissolved upon a two-thirds affirmative vote of the entire membership at any regular or special meeting, provided that written notice of the proposed amendment or proposed dissolution has been given to each member at least fourteen (14) days prior to such meeting. On dissolution, all debts and expenses of the association shall first be paid, and the remaining assets of the association shall be distributed to the membership in cash or in kind, or partly in cash and partly in kind, ratably apportioned in accordance with the capital accounts of the members.

IN WITNESS WHEREOF, the founding members have signed and executed these Articles of Association the _____ day of _____ , _____ , at _____ (City and state) _____ .

_____

_____

_____

_____

*Note:* All founding members must sign this document.

# SAMPLE PARTNERSHIP AGREEMENT

Agreement made this _____ day of _____ , _____ , between _____ (name and address of each partner) _____ , herein referred to as the partners.

1. **Name.**  The name of the partnership shall be

_____ .

2. **Purpose.**  The purpose of the partnership shall be to educate the partners in securities evaluation and for investment through periodic contributions by the partners for their mutual benefit, and to do all other acts incidental thereto pursuant to the law of the State of _____ .

3. **Duration.**  The partnership shall commence as of_____ , _____ , and shall continue until it is dis-solved as hereinafter provided.

4. **Meetings.**  Regular meetings of the partners shall be held from time to time as determined by the partners. Special meetings may be called at any time by a majority of the partners.

5. **Capital Contributions.**  Each partner shall contribute $ _____ as his or her initial capital contribution to the assets of the partnership. Each partner shall be required to make a

of the partnership. Each partner shall be required to make a monthly contribution to the partnership in an amount to be determined by vote of the partners.

6. **Capital Accounts.** A capital account shall be maintained in the name of each partner. Any increase or decrease in the value of the partnership on any valuation date shall be either credited or debited, respectively, to the capital account of each partner in proportion to the value of that partner's capital account on said date. Each partner's contribution to, or withdrawal from, the partnership shall be credited or debited, respectively, to that partner's capital account.

7. **Management**

a. *General policies.* Partners shall have an interest in the conduct of the affairs of the partnership in proportion to their capital contribution. Except as otherwise provided in this agreement, all decisions shall be by a majority vote of the partners.

b. *Election of officers.* For convenience in the transaction of the business of the partnership, there shall be elected from among the partners a presiding partner, an assisting presiding partner, a recording partner and a financial partner. Before the opening of partnership business, these officers shall be elected at a meeting of the partners. The officers shall serve for such terms as may be prescribed by resolution of the partners and until their successors are duly elected and qualified. The partners, by resolution, may require that a fidelity bond be secured at partnership expense covering the fidelity of any officer. Any officer may be removed by two-thirds vote of the partners during his or her term of office for neglect of responsibility or for malfeasance in office.

c. *Duties of officers.* The presiding partner shall preside at all meetings and shall serve as the chief executive officer of the partnership.

The *assisting presiding partner* shall perform the duties of presiding partner in the absence or incapacity of the presiding partner.

The *recording partner* shall have custody of and maintain the records of the partnership and shall prepare and maintain written minutes of the meetings and decisions taken by the partnership.

the name of the partnership necessary bank depository accounts and shall make monthly reports to the partners as to the financial condition of the partnership. The partners, by resolution, may designate one or more officers, in addition to the financial partner, who may withdraw funds from the partnership bank accounts. The financial partner shall maintain written accounts of the transactions of the partnership, which shall at all reasonable times be available to any member for examination. No less than annually, the financial partner shall furnish to each partner a full and complete written accounting of the assets and liabilities of the partnership, and of the capital accounts of each partner.

In addition to the above enumerated duties, the officers shall perform such other duties as are commonly associated with their offices or as directed by resolution of the partners.

8. **Fees and Compensation.**   No partner shall be compensated for services rendered to the partnership. However, responsible and necessary partnership expenses shall be reimbursed by the partnership.

9. **Bank Accounts.**   The partnership shall maintain checking and other accounts in such bank or banks as may be agreed on by the partners, and funds deposited in such account(s) shall be withdrawn by check signed by either of (Number) partners designated by the partnership.

10. **Securities Broker.**   The partners shall by resolution select a securities broker to execute orders placed by the authorized officers of the partnership. The broker shall not be a member of the partnership. The partners by appropriate resolution shall designate the officer or officers of the partnership authorized to purchase or sell securities through the broker, and the broker may rely upon such resolution until it is modified, changed or rescinded in writing. Stocks, bonds and securities owned by the partnership shall be registered in the partnership name, or in the names of one or more officers as trustees for the partnership, or may be left with the broker to be held in the "street name" (registered in the name of the brokerage firm) for the account of the partnership. Any corporation or transfer agent called upon to transfer securities to or from the name of the partnership or a trustee for the partnership may rely upon instructions or assign-

ments signed by a designated officer or officers of the partnership.

11. **Profits and Losses.**   Net profits and losses of the partnership shall be shared by the partners in proportion to their respective capital accounts.

12. **Admission of New Partners.**   Additional partners may be admitted at any time by unanimous consent of all partners. As a condition of partnership, all partners agree to be bound by the terms of this Partnership Agreement and by all resolutions adopted or to be adopted by vote of the partners.

13. **Withdrawal or Death of Partners.**   A partner may withdraw from the partnership at any time. A withdrawing partner shall give written notice to the partnership's recording partner or any other officer. The effective date of such withdrawal shall be as of the next regularly scheduled partnership meeting. The date for valuation of the withdrawing partner's interest shall be the first regular meeting following the meeting at which notice of withdrawal is received. Between receipt of the notice of withdrawal and the subsequent withdrawal valuation date, the other partners shall have the option to purchase, in proportion to their capital accounts in the partnership, the capital account of the withdrawing partner. If the other partners do not elect to purchase the capital account of the withdrawing partner by such valuation date, the partnership shall use cash on hand or sell sufficient securities to pay the withdrawing partner the value of his or her capital account, less the actual cost of selling sufficient securities to obtain the cash necessary to meet the withdrawal. The withdrawing partner shall be paid in cash, but without interest, not later than 90 days after such valuation date. Death or legal incapacity of a partner shall be handled in the same manner as a voluntary withdrawal.

14. **Nonassignability of Partners' Interest.**   No member may assign, transfer, pledge or hypothecate his or her partnership or capital account, in whole or in part, and any attempt to do so shall be construed as such partner's election to withdraw from the partnership.

15. **Limitation of Authority of Partners.**   No partners shall:

   a. Have the right or authority to bind or obligate the partnership to any extent whatsoever with regard to any matter outside the scope of the partnership business;

b. Assign, transfer, pledge, mortgage or sell all or part of his or her interest in the partnership to any other partner or person whomever without the unanimous consent of all other partners;

c. Purchase an investment for the partnership where less than the full purchase price is paid for same without the unanimous consent of all other partners;

d. Use the partnership name, credit or property for other than duly-authorized partnership purposes;

e. Do any act detrimental to the interests of the partnership or which would make it impossible to carry on the business or affairs of the partnership.

16. **Quorum, Amendments and Dissolution.** A quorum for the transaction of business shall be two-thirds of the membership of the partnership, and the election of officers and the transaction of other business shall be by a majority of the partners present and voting, providing a quorum is present. This agreement may be amended or the partnership may be dissolved upon a two-thirds affirmative vote of all partners at any regular or special meeting, provided that written notice of the proposed amendment or proposed dissolution has been given to each partner at least fourteen (14) days prior to such meeting. On dissolution, all debts and expenses of the partnership shall first be paid, and the remaining assets of the partnership shall be distributed to the partners in cash or in kind, or partly in cash and partly in kind, ratably apportioned in accordance with the capital accounts of the partners.

IN WITNESS WHEREOF, the undersigned parties have executed this agreement at _____ (Location) _____

_____ this _____ day of

_____ , _____ .

_____

_____

_____

_____

*Note:* All partners must sign this document.

# INDEX

Please complete and send to:  Kathryn Shaw
                               P.O. Box 359
                               Victor, Montana 59875

☐  Yes, I am interested in starting an investment club or joining an existing club in my area.

☐  Yes, my investment club would like to increase its membership.

You have my permission to contact other club enthusiasts and give them my name as a possible candidate for membership.

Name _____

Street address _____

City _____ State _____ ZIP _____

Telephone ( ___ ) _____

My home is within 10–20 miles of _____
(nearest town of size)

The author will act as a clearinghouse for prospective investment club members. Your name will be kept on file for two years, and you will be referred to other respondents in your geographic area.